DVD VIDEO INCLUDES 2 DVDs

Mastering the Modes for the Rock Guitarist

By Dave Celentano and Steve Gorenberg

Ionian

Dorian

Phrygian

Lydian

Mixolydian

Aeolian

Locrian

ISBN 978-1-6037-8963-9

HAL•LEONARD® CORPORATION

7777 W. BLUEMOUND RD. P.O. BOX 13819 MILWAUKEE, WI 53213

Visit Hal Leonard Online at
www.halleonard.com

CONTENTS

INTRODUCTION

Learning the modes is an essential part of mastering the guitar. Many students will learn and memorize the modal scales but still find themselves confused as to how these scales can be applied to their playing. With this book and the accompanying DVDs, we'll give you a solid tutorial on each of the modes and how they can be used to create interesting solos, rhythms, and riffs. Each mode is given its own chapter that follows along with the DVD and contains beginner, intermediate, and advanced solos, as well as a rhythm track for you to solo over. The theory behind the use of the modes is discussed extensively, and we'll show you how to apply this knowledge to your playing, giving you a thorough foundation on modal theory using hands-on examples in rock, metal, and blues. All of the scale positions are demonstrated on the DVD, and each of the solos is played at regular and slow tempos and then broken down lick by lick for you. Each chapter in this book follows the DVD program and also contains additional content, such as harmonic analysis and three-octave scales. There's also an additional section at the end of the book showing the modes in other keys, plus a section containing all of the rhythm tracks for easy reference.

While we strongly encourage you to work through this entire book, you can also use it as a reference guide for each individual mode. It's all here just waiting to be tapped into. In addition, the accompanying rhythm backing tracks should not only be used for practicing the solos we've provided, but for you to jam over and rehearse your own modal inspirations. These isolated rhythm tracks can all be found at the end of the DVD program. So grab your favorite guitar, and let's get started!

ABOUT THE AUTHORS

Dave Celentano is a freelance guitarist, music transcriber, composer, author, and educator living in southern California. After graduating from G.I.T. at Musician's Institute, he began writing educational guitar books, transcription books, videos, and DVDs for Centerstream Publications, Star Licks, Hal Leonard Corp., Music Sales, and Cherry Lane Music, and since then he's written for numerous other publications. Dave was a part of legendary German guitarist Michael Schenker's first educational DVD, *The Legendary Guitar of Michael Schenker*, providing the instructional content and transcribing Michael's licks. Dave has released two solo CDs, *Guitar Stew* and *Wicked Music Box*, and one with his former band Sir Real, *Johari's Window*, all available through his web site www.davecelentano.com. Some of his work with Cherry Lane Music includes the DVD *Mastering the Modes for Rock Guitar* and recording the audio CD companions for the books *Stylistic History of Heavy Metal*, *Joe Satriani's Guitar Secrets*, and *Guitar Secrets*.

Steve Gorenberg is a music educator, author, arranger, transcriber and engraver based in Los Angeles. After earning a B.S. in Music and Sound Recording, Steve joined Cherry Lane Music's print division as a transcriber and in-house music editor. He has since continued as a freelance transcriber, editor, and engraver for Cherry Lane Music, *Guitar for the Practicing Musician* magazine, Hal Leonard Corp., Fred Russell Publishing, and Warner Bros. Inc., and has edited, co-written and designed numerous music education products. To date, Steve has created thousands of official note-for-note guitar and bass transcriptions for artists including Metallica, Guns N' Roses, the Red Hot Chili Peppers, the Rolling Stones, Van Halen, Pearl Jam, Rush, Black Sabbath, Queen and John Mayer.

ACKNOWLEDGMENTS

Much thanks goes out to Cherry Lane's top dog John Stix and editor Mark Phillips, who together made this book possible. Also, extra special thanks to my family and the many awesome teachers and mentors I've had.

– *Dave Celentano*

Thanks to Mark Phillips and John Stix of Cherry Lane Music, as well as Jeff Schroedl and Denis Kavemeier at Hal Leonard for helping to make this book possible. Special thanks to my family and friends for their never ending support, and especially to my students and the entire music community for their inspiration over the years.

– *Steve Gorenberg*

GETTING STARTED

A mode is an inversion of a scale. The most common modes are the scales that are built on each individual step of the major scale. There are seven different notes in a major scale; therefore, there are seven modes—one for each step of the scale. For this first section, we'll briefly explore the modes and the theory behind them using the key of C. The C major scale contains only natural notes (no sharps or flats), so all of the modes derived from the key of C will also contain only natural notes. Let's take a look at one octave of the C major scale, beginning at the 8th fret on the 6th string. The scale diagram below represents a section of the fretboard beginning at the 7th fret (7th position); the lowest horizontal line represents the 6th string, and the top line represents the 1st string. The circled numbers in the scale diagram indicate the suggested fingering for playing the scale; the black circles in the scale diagram indicate the tonic (root note) C. The major scale is also known as the *Ionian* mode, the mode built on the tonic of the major key.

C Major Scale (Ionian)

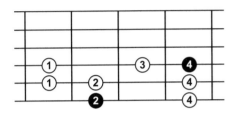

7 fr.

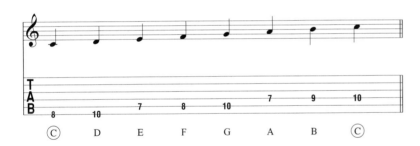

The tonal quality and characteristics of a scale (major sounding, minor sounding, etc.) are created by the series of whole steps and half steps that make up that scale's formula. On the guitar, a whole step is the distance of two frets; a half step is the distance of one fret.

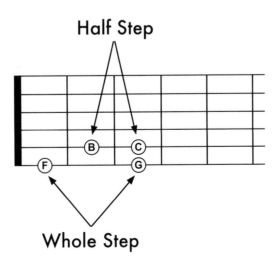

Here's the half step and whole step formula for the C major scale (or Ionian mode). In all major scales, half steps occur between the 3rd and 4th steps and between the 7th and 8th steps of the scale. All of the other intervals in the major scale are whole steps.

whole step	whole step	half step	whole step	whole step	whole step	half step
C	D	E	F	G	A	B	C

Now let's take the C major scale in 7th position from the previous page and expand it to a two-octave scale.

Two-Octave C Major Scale

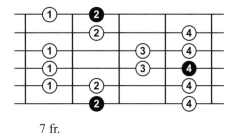

7 fr.

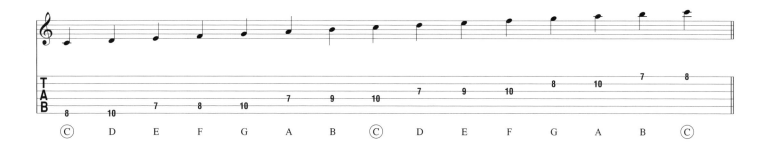

If we were to play from D to the octave D using all of the notes in the C major scale, this would give us our second mode: the *Dorian* mode. We're still using all of the same notes as the key of C major, but now we're considering D to be the tonic instead of C. This will give us an entirely new series of half steps and whole steps. Now the half steps occur between the 2nd and 3rd steps and between the 6th and 7th steps.

whole step	half step	whole step	whole step	whole step	half step	whole step
D	E	F	G	A	B	C	D

Utilizing the notes above, the following scale diagram, notation, and tab show one octave of the D Dorian scale. Since D is now considered the root note, the D's have been indicated using black circles in the scale diagram.

Mastering the Modes for the Rock Guitarist

D Dorian Scale

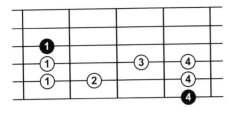

7 fr.

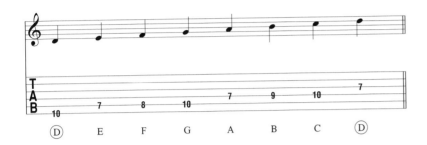

Using this same method we can continue to build a new modal scale on every step of the C major scale, each with its own unique series of half steps and whole steps. The remaining modes, in order, are the *Phrygian, Lydian, Mixolydian, Aeolian,* and *Locrian* modes. The chart below shows each mode's formula of half steps and whole steps. On the following page, we'll continue to show one octave of each mode in 7th position using scale diagrams, notation, and tab.

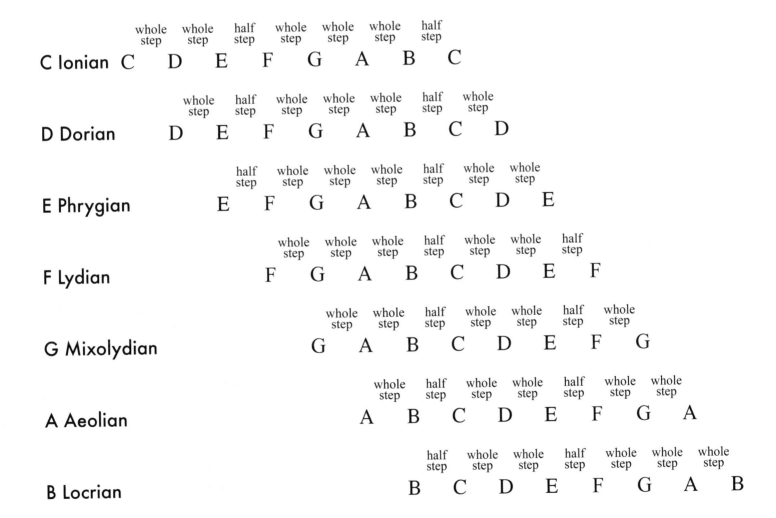

E Phrygian Scale

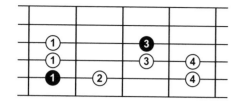

7 fr.

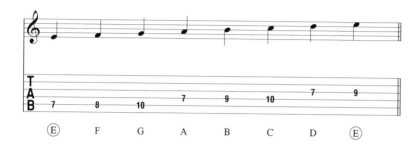

E   F   G   A   B   C   D   E

F Lydian Scale

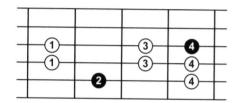

7 fr.

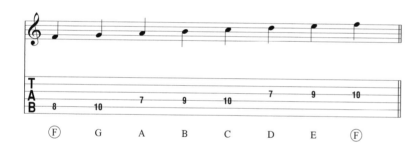

F   G   A   B   C   D   E   F

G Mixolydian Scale

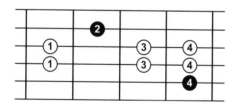

7 fr.

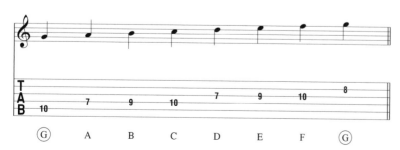

G   A   B   C   D   E   F   G

Just as the Ionian scale is the same as the major scale, the Aeolian scale is the same as the minor scale. Since A minor (Aeolian) and C major both contain all natural notes (no sharps or flats), A minor is referred to as the *relative minor* to C major. If you've already mastered the major and minor scales on guitar prior to learning the modes, then you already know your Ionian and Aeolian scales.

A Aeolian Scale

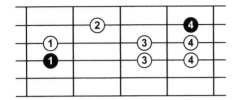

7 fr.

The Locrian mode is the most dissonant of all the modes. It contains a flatted 2nd and a flatted 5th, giving it a diminished quality.

B Locrian Scale

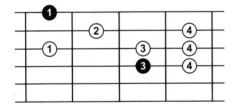

7 fr.

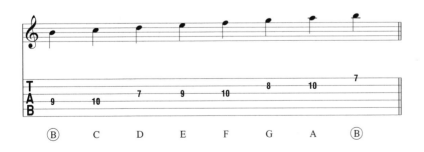

We can also build chords on each step of the major scale, giving us all of the basic chords to create chord progressions and rhythms in that key. Simple major and minor chords contain three different notes and are referred to as triads. These three notes are determined by starting with any note in the scale and adding every third note of the scale above it, creating intervals of 3rds. To build a C major chord, start with the note C, then add E (the third note up from C) and then G (the third note up from E). The note C is called the root note of the chord (the note that gives the chord its letter name). E is referred to as the 3rd of the chord because it is three scale steps up from the root note, and G is referred to as the 5th of the chord because it is five scale steps up from the root note.

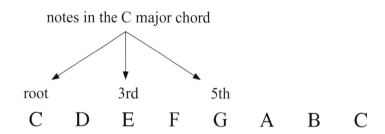

The distance in pitch between the root note of the chord and the 3rd determines whether that chord is major or minor. A major 3rd is the distance of two whole steps from the root note; a minor 3rd is one and a half steps from the root note. All of the chords built on the steps of the major scale are either major or minor with the exception of the chord built on the seventh step of the scale, which contains a ♭5, making it a diminished chord. The music notation below shows each of the triads built on the steps of the C major scale.

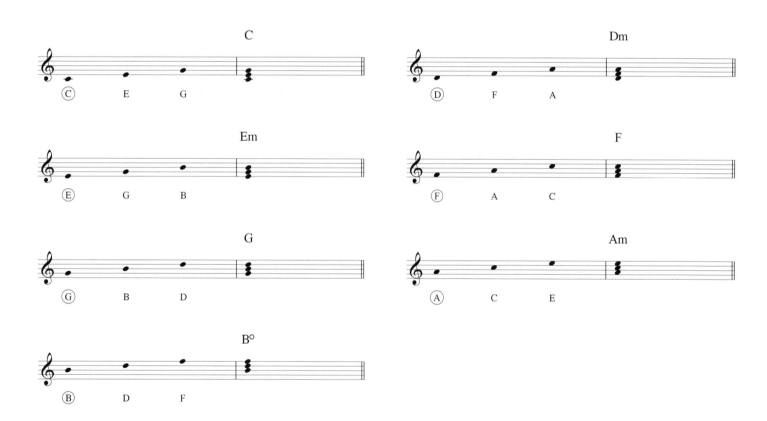

You can use any combination of the notes in a triad to create chords on the guitar. The following example uses notation, tab, and chord frames to show some common voicings for these chords. Roman numeral analysis has been added above the chord frames and is commonly used to refer to the different chords in a key. Upper case Roman numerals indicate major chords, while lower case Roman numerals refer to minor and diminished chords.

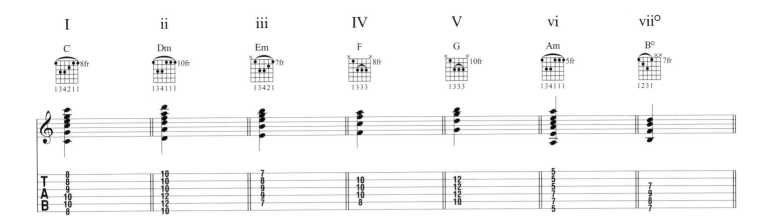

We can add an additional 3rd above each of the previous chords to create the seventh chords. The I and IV chords become major seventh chords, the V chord becomes a dominant seventh chord, the ii, iii, and vi chords become minor seventh chords, and the vii° chord becomes a minor seventh flat-five chord. The following examples show the seventh chords in notation in the key of C major, as well as some common voicings for guitar on the staff below.

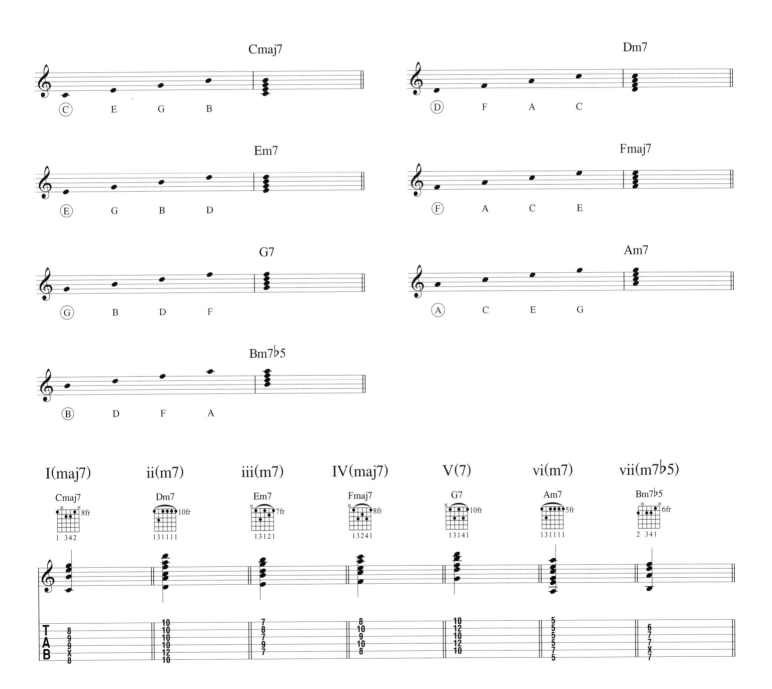

Before continuing on to the next chapter, let's compare the different modal scales to help us get a better understanding of their tonality and how they can be applied while soloing. The basic tonality of a scale—whether it's generally a major or minor sounding scale—is determined by the 3rd step of the scale. The Ionian, Lydian, and Mixolydian scales all contain major 3rds, while the rest of the modes contain minor 3rds. The chart below shows the modes relative to the key of C with a numerical analysis of their intervals (compared to the major scale) and the major and minor 3rds indicated above using brackets.

		⌐— major third —⌐						
	1	2	3	4	5	6	7	8
C Ionian	C	D	E	F	G	A	B	C

		⌐— minor third —⌐						
	1	2	♭3	4	5	6	♭7	8
D Dorian		D	E	F	G	A	B	C	D

		⌐— minor third —⌐						
	1	♭2	♭3	4	5	♭6	♭7	8
E Phrygian			E	F	G	A	B	C	D	E

			⌐— major third —⌐					
	1	2	3	♯4	5	6	7	8
F Lydian			F	G	A	B	C	D	E	F

			⌐— major third —⌐					
	1	2	3	4	5	6	♭7	8
G Mixolydian			G	A	B	C	D	E	F	G

			⌐— minor third —⌐					
	1	2	♭3	4	5	♭6	♭7	8
A Aeolian			A	B	C	D	E	F	G	A

			⌐— minor third —⌐					
	1	♭2	♭3	4	♭5	♭6	♭7	8
B Locrian			B	C	D	E	F	G	A	B

Now let's compare the Ionian scale with the Lydian and Mixolydian scales transposed so that C is the root note (tonic) of each scale. Notice how similar the C Lydian and C Mixolydian scales are to the C Ionian (major) scale—only one note in each scale differs from the major scale. The Lydian scale contains a sharped 4th, while the Mixolydian scale contains a flatted 7th. Getting to know these basic similarities between the scales will help you to demystify and recognize the modes and give you some ideas on how to substitute them when you're soloing in major and minor keys. If you've already perfected your major and minor scales, knowing these slight differences will make it much easier to memorize and master the rest of the modes.

	1	2	3	4	5	6	7	8
Ionian (Major)	C	D	E	F	G	A	B	C

	1	2	3	♯4	5	6	7	8
Lydian	C	D	E	F♯	G	A	B	C

	1	2	3	4	5	6	♭7	8
Mixolydian	C	D	E	F	G	A	B♭	C

The following are the scale diagrams, notation, and tab for one octave of the three major sounding modes, all using C at the 8th fret of the 6th string as the tonic so that you can directly compare them on the fretboard. The ♯4 of the Lydian scale and the ♭7 of the Mixolydian scale have been indicated using grey circles on the scale diagrams.

C Ionian Scale (Major)

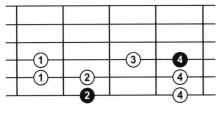

7 fr.

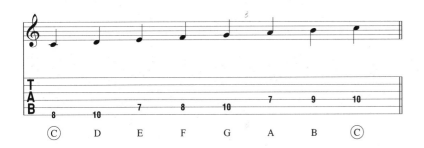

C Lydian Scale

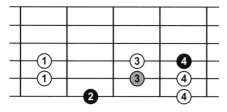

7 fr.

C   D   E   F♯   G   A   B   C

C Mixolydian Scale

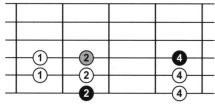

7 fr.

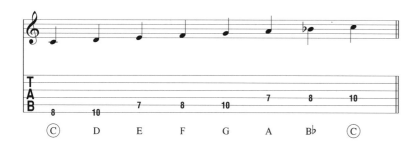

C   D   E   F   G   A   B♭   C

Now let's compare the remaining modes with the Aeolian (natural minor) scale, only this time let's use A minor (the relative minor to C major) since it contains all natural notes. The A Dorian scale is very similar and only differs with a sharped 6th. The A Phrygian mode is also the same as the minor scale except for a flatted 2nd. The A Locrian scale is not used as often since it contains both a flatted 2nd and a flatted 5th, giving it a diminished sound. The Locrian mode is something you would encounter in riffs from metal bands like Metallica or Slayer, due to its dark and somewhat evil sounding tonality. Locrian is closely related to the Phrygian scale since both contain the ♭2 and only differ with the Locrian's addition of the ♭5.

	1	2	b3	4	5	b6	b7	8
Aeolian (Minor)	A	B	C	D	E	F	G	A

	1	2	b3	4	5	6	b7	8
Dorian	A	B	C	D	E	F♯	G	A

	1	b2	b3	4	5	b6	b7	8
Phrygian	A	Bb	C	D	E	F	G	A

	1	b2	b3	4	b5	b6	b7	8
Locrian	A	Bb	C	D	Eb	F	G	A

Here are the minor sounding modes all shown in one octave starting at A on the 6th string, 5th fret. As before, all of the notes in the Dorian, Phrygian, and Locrian scales that differ from the natural minor scale have been indicated using grey circles on the scale diagrams. Once you've got a basic understanding of modal theory and you've memorized the names of the modes and how they relate to each other, continue on to the following chapters where we'll explore each individual mode in depth using different scale positions, modal rhythms, and lead examples in many styles.

A Aeolian Scale (Minor)

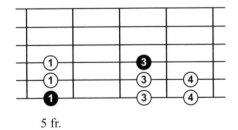

5 fr.

A Dorian Scale

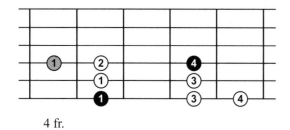

4 fr.

A   B   C   D   E   F♯   G   A

A Phrygian Scale

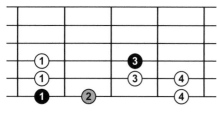

5 fr.

A   B♭   C   D   E   F   G   A

A Locrian Scale

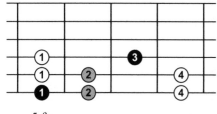

5 fr.

A   B♭   C   D   E♭   F   G   A

IONIAN MODE

Ioninan Scale Patterns

The first mode we're going to cover in detail is the Ionian mode. As we discussed in the previous chapter, the Ionian mode is identical to the major scale; it has a happy and light-hearted sound, mostly due to the major third and major seventh intervals. If you already know your major scale positions, this will be a good review before continuing on to the Ionian rhythm and solo examples.

In each of the following chapters, the scales, rhythms, and solos will be shown with A as the root note, making it easier for us to compare the different modes. All of the scale patterns will be presented in closed position (no open strings) so that you can transpose them to any key. Each scale will be shown ascending and descending in five positions, essentially covering a full octave of the fretboard. The scale patterns in the lower portion of the fretboard can also be played one octave higher by moving the pattern up 12 frets. All of the root notes (the A's) are indicated on the scale diagrams using black circles and are also circled under the tab staves. Each scale position will begin on a different note of the scale, allowing us to take full advantage of all of the notes available in the key in that particular position. For example, the first pattern below begins with F♯ on the 6th string, 2nd fret.

Ionian Scale Pattern #1

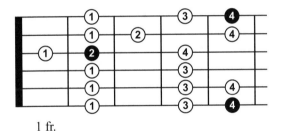

1 fr.

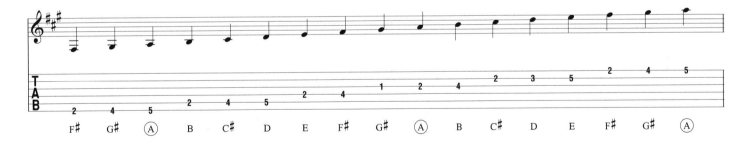

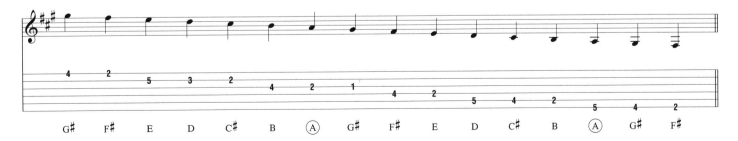

Ionian Scale Pattern #2

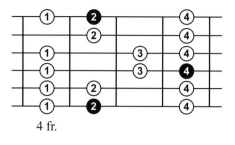

4 fr.

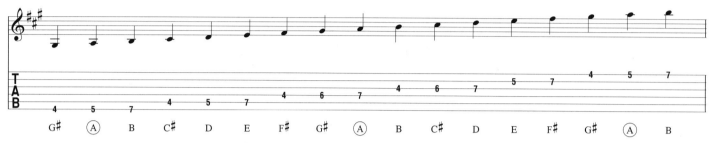

G# Ⓐ B C# D E F# G# Ⓐ B C# D E F# G# Ⓐ B

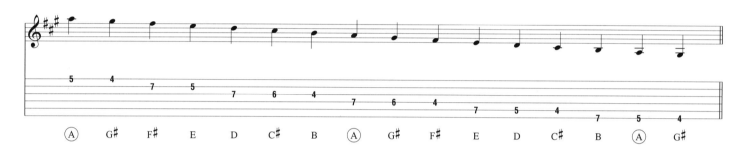

Ⓐ G# F# E D C# B Ⓐ G# F# E D C# B Ⓐ G#

Ionian Scale Pattern #3

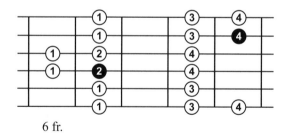

6 fr.

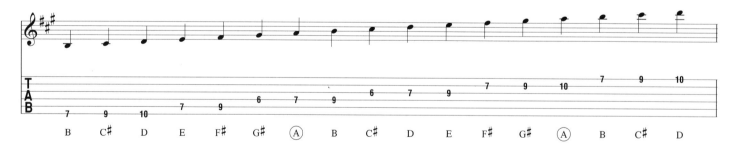

B C# D E F# G# Ⓐ B C# D E F# G# Ⓐ B C# D

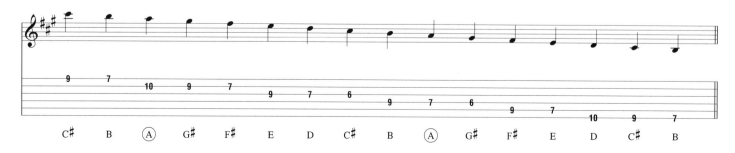

C# B Ⓐ G# F# E D C# B Ⓐ G# F# E D C# B

Ionian Scale Pattern #4

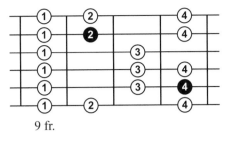

9 fr.

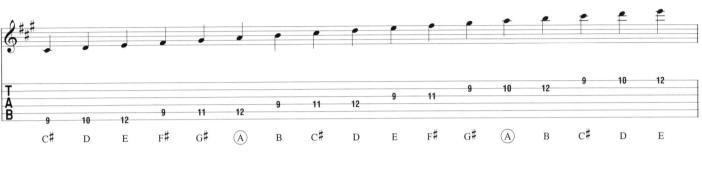

C# D E F# G# (A) B C# D E F# G# (A) B C# D E

D C# B (A) G# F# E D C# B (A) G# F# E D C#

Ionian Scale Pattern #5

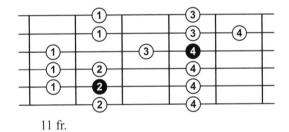

11 fr.

E F# G# (A) B C# D E F# G# (A) B C# D E F#

E D C# B (A) G# F# E D C# B (A) G# F# E

Ioninan Solos

Beginner Solo

For each mode we'll show examples of three short solos—beginner, intermediate, and advanced—all over the same rhythm track. These solos are played at slow and regular tempos and broken down by phrase on the accompanying DVD. The section at the end of the DVD contains all of the isolated rhythm tracks so you can play these solos over them and then try some of your own. Our first beginner solo combines a few different scale positions and is reminiscent of melodic solos in the style of the Beatles.

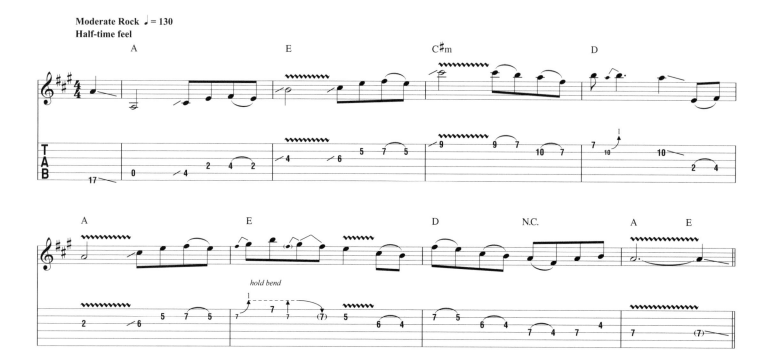

Intermediate Solo

The following intermediate solo is in the style of something Boston might play over an Ionian rhythm. It contains a few more useful techniques like the hammer-on double-stops in the last few measures.

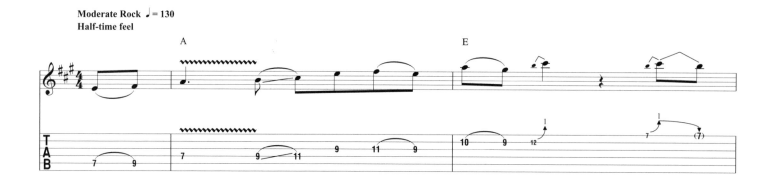

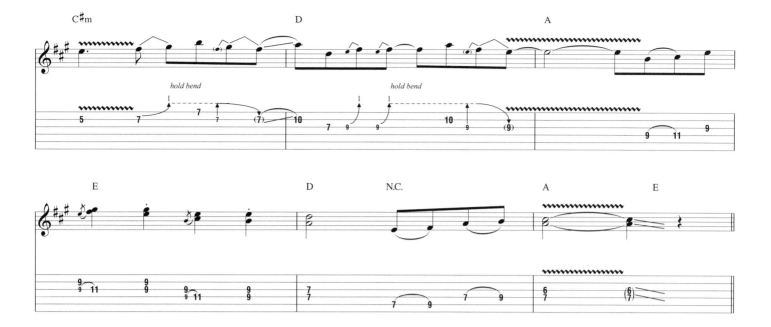

Advanced Solo

Now let's move on to a more complex solo along the lines of something Joe Satriani might play. It's made up of triplet phrases using hammer-ons and pull-offs and includes moves up into the higher register of the neck. Since all three solos are played over the same rhythm track, they can be combined into one long, continuous solo.

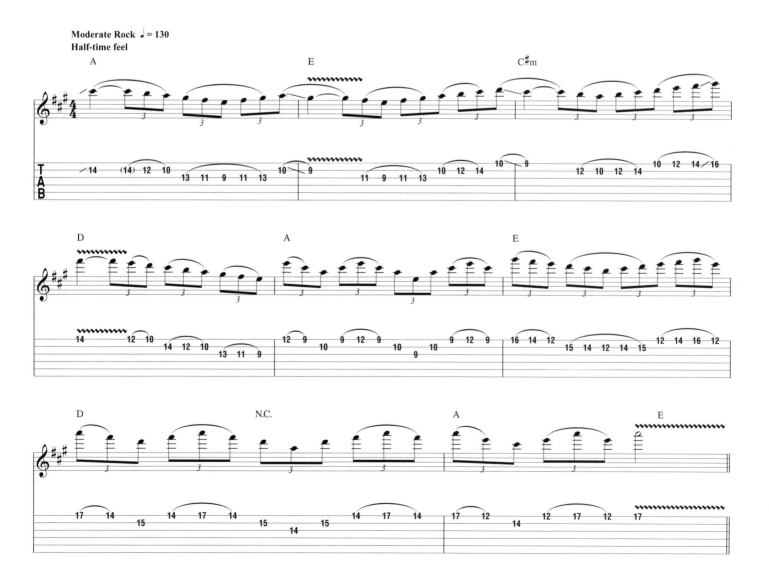

Ioninan Rhythm

Let's harmonize the A Ionian scale and see what chords are available for creating rhythms in this key. We'll begin with the major, minor, and diminished triads, followed by the barre chords demonstrated on the DVD. These are all moveable chord forms and can be transposed to other Ionian keys as well.

Now let's take a look at the rhythm track that's being played behind the previous solos. It utilizes some of the chord voicings that were shown above, but all of the chords are in the key of A Ionian. The progression uses the standard I, IV, and V chords (A, D, and E), as well as the iii chord (C♯m). This is a fairly basic chord progression played at a medium tempo, giving you a solid rhythm track to try out your own solos using the Ionian scales.

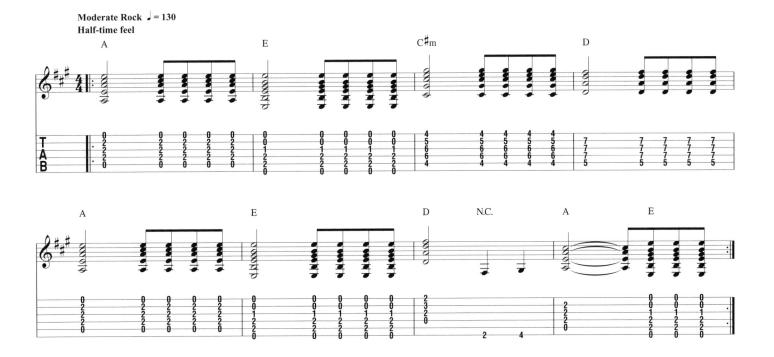

It's good to know a few more useful voicings for the chords in A Ionian. The following example shows some common options to choose from when creating progressions in this key. Some of these are open chords and are only applicable here, but all of the closed position chords can be transposed to other keys.

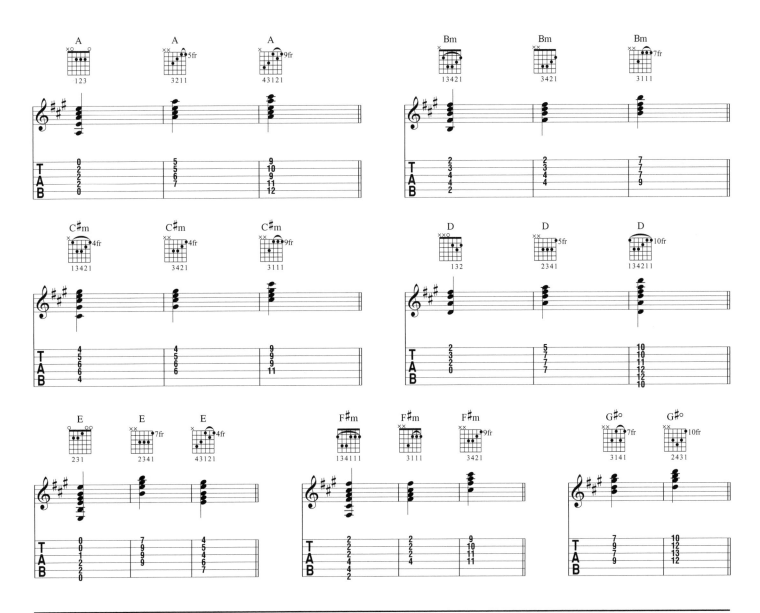

Here are the seventh chords for the harmonized Ionian scale. Some suggested chord voicings are included below.

Three-Octave Ionian Scales

The purpose of learning the five different scale patterns is to get you to visualize the scale across the entire fretboard. However, most proficient players won't stay in one position for an entire solo. Learning to move seamlessly from position to position will allow you to play more interesting solos across a wider range. This was demonstrated in all three of the previous solos. There are endless possibilities for moving around the fretboard by pivoting positions and using slides; here are just a few examples and suggested fingerings for playing the scale across three full octaves.

The first example below shows both the ascending and descending scale with various points along the string you can use to slide up or down from one position to the next. As a suggestion, we've indicated that you should try to perform the ascending and descending slides using your first finger. You may find this economy of motion to be most comfortable, but you're welcome to experiment and decide what works best for you. Many players prefer to perform ascending slides with the 3rd or 4th finger, depending on the context. One way to help remember the pattern is to remember the number of notes per string. Ascending, the amount of notes per string is 4-4-3-4-3-4.

Ascending

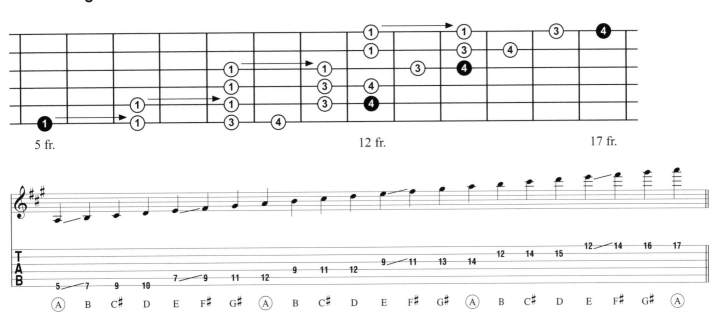

Descending

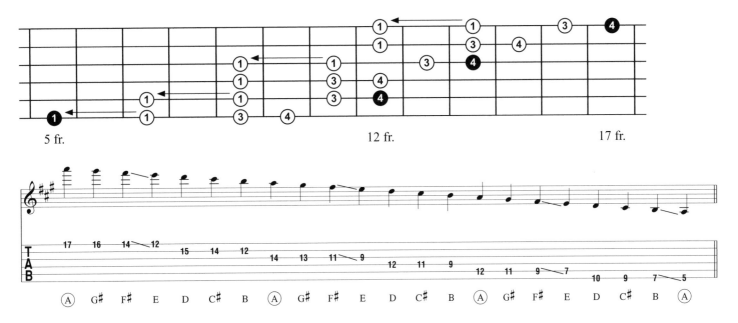

Here's a second version of the three octave scale that incorporates wide stretches using the 1st, 2nd, and 4th fingers. Initially, this may seem more difficult compared to the previous example, but once you're comfortable with the finger span you can attain great speed and accuracy with this technique, especially when employing quick hammer-ons and pull-offs. The number of notes per string in this variation is 3-4-3-4-4-4.

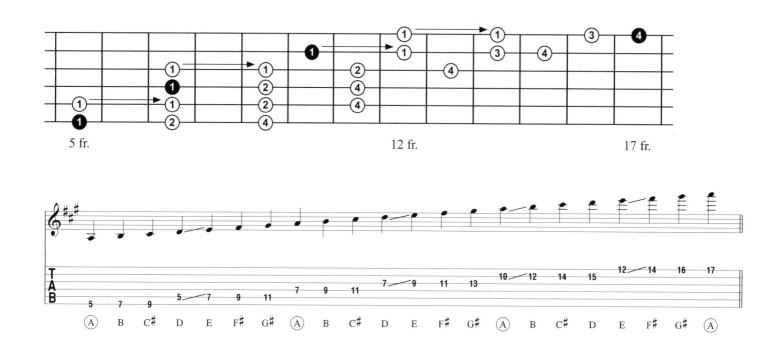

Finally, here's a third way to play the three octave scale without slides. By shifting from larger portions of the scale positions in convenient places, you can split the fretboard up into three distinct sections. These sections are indicated using brackets above the notation staff below. An easy way to remember the pattern is to compare the last part of the fingering from the first section to the start of the fingering in the next section. On the 4th string in 4th position, the fingering is 1-3-4. Then just move your hand up to 9th position and repeat the 1-3-4 finger pattern to begin the next section of the scale. This type of mirrored fingering happens again with the 1-2-4 fingering on the 2nd string, before switching up to the 14th fret and repeating the same 1-2-4 finger pattern.

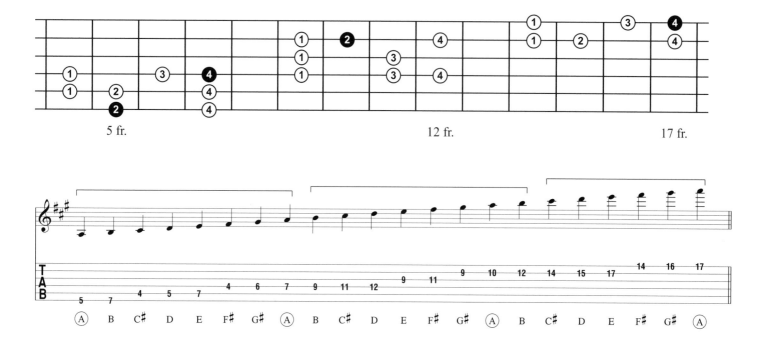

DORIAN MODE

Dorian Scale Patterns

The Dorian mode is a popular minor-sounding mode. The raised 6th is what sets it apart from the typical natural minor scale, making it an ideal choice for creating interesting riffs and solos. David Gilmour's guitar solo in "Another Brick in the Wall, Part 2" is a good example of a Dorian solo. Carlos Santana also uses the Dorian mode in many of his solos. Newer examples of the Dorian mode can be found in the main riffs of songs by Soundgarden and the main chorus riff of the Filter song, "Hey Man, Nice Shot," where the raised 6th clearly stands out in the second measure.

Since we're presenting all of the modes in this book using A as the root note, we must first determine what the key signature is for A Dorian, which will tell us what notes are in the scale. The Dorian mode is built on the second step of the major scale, and the note A is the second step of the G major scale. Therefore G major is the relative major key to A Dorian. The key of G major contains one sharp (F♯), and all of the other notes are natural notes. If we play all of these notes starting with A (A-B-C-D-E-F♯-G-A), that will give us the A Dorian scale. The following five scale patterns show the A Dorian scale played across the entire fretboard. As before, the black circled notes on the scale diagrams represent the root note A.

Dorian Scale Pattern #1

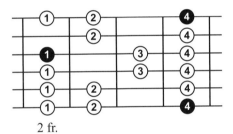

2 fr.

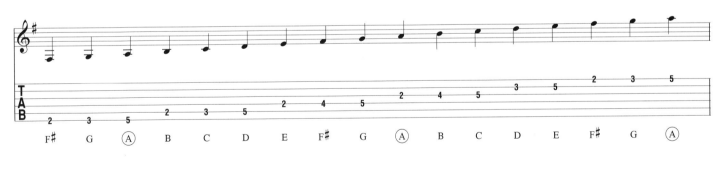

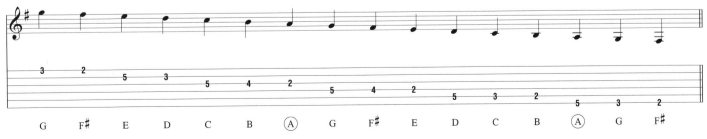

Dorian Scale Pattern #2

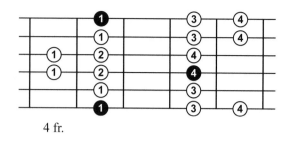

4 fr.

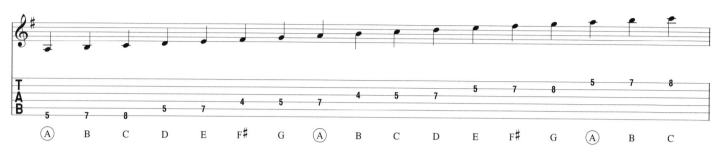

| A | B | C | D | E | F# | G | A | B | C | D | E | F# | G | A | B | C |

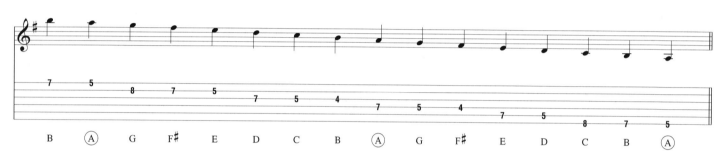

| B | A | G | F# | E | D | C | B | A | G | F# | E | D | C | B | A |

Dorian Scale Pattern #3

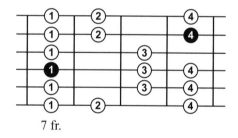

7 fr.

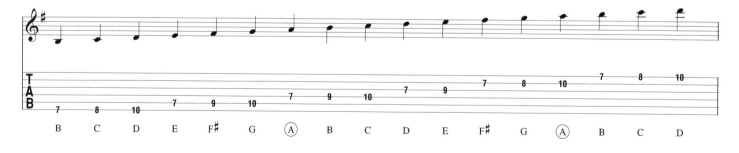

| B | C | D | E | F# | G | A | B | C | D | E | F# | G | A | B | C | D |

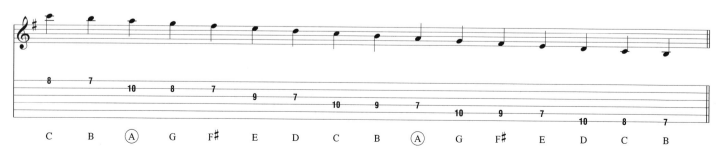

| C | B | A | G | F# | E | D | C | B | A | G | F# | E | D | C | B |

Dorian Scale Pattern #4

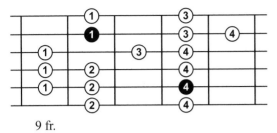

9 fr.

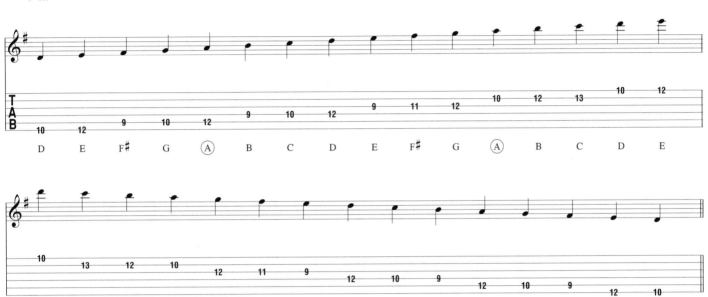

D E F# G (A) B C D E F# G (A) B C D E

D C B (A) G F# E D C B (A) G F# E D

Dorian Scale Pattern #5

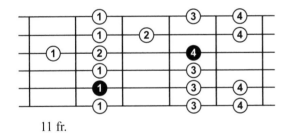

11 fr.

E F# G (A) B C D E F# G (A) B C D E F# G

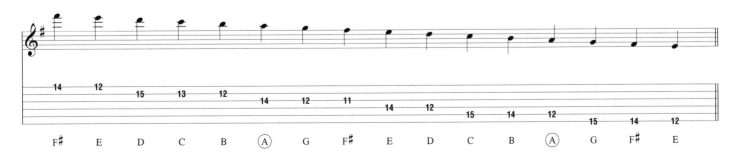

F# E D C B (A) G F# E D C B (A) G F# E

Dorian Solos

Beginner Solo

This beginner level solo is reminiscent of solos in the style of the Allman Brothers Band. Most of it is centered around the 4th position on the fretboard, the solo then travels up to the 7th position where the Dorian tonality becomes apparent. Refer to the DVD for a demonstration of the proper techniques and fingering for these solos.

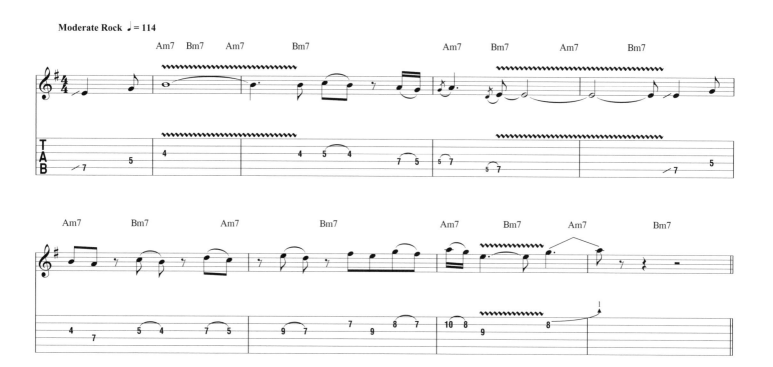

Intermediate Solo

Now let's move on to the intermediate solo in the style of something Mick Taylor might have played with the Rolling Stones. This example is based on a melodic bend and release motif that is repeated and varied in a call and response style, followed by some syncopated bends, and ends in a series of unison bends. On its own, there really isn't anything in this solo to distinguish it as Dorian besides the rhythm part that's being played underneath it because the note F♯ isn't used at all in the solo. This is a good example of how the progression alone may determine what the modal key is—something we'll discuss further when we break down the rhythm track later in this chapter.

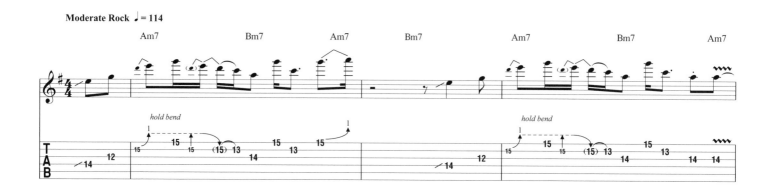

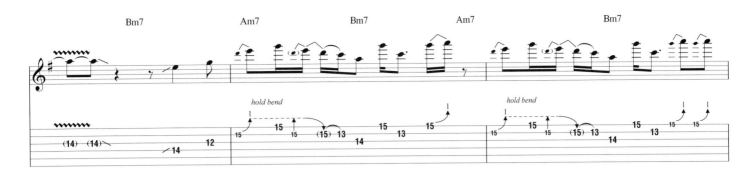

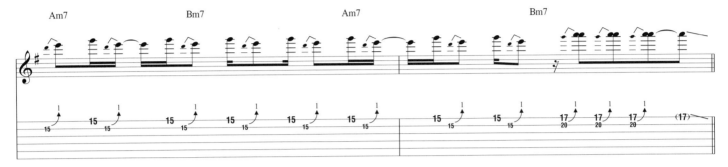

Advanced Solo

Now let's move on to a Carlos Santana style advanced Dorian solo. Here, the Dorian tonality really comes alive through the use of plenty of F♯'s that distinguish the solo from a regular minor scale solo. You can hear it right away in the first two measures during the rapid series of pull-offs. The solo then moves down the neck to resolve directly on an F♯ at the 4th fret, which employs a half-bend and release before sliding off the note. The section that follows in measure 5 on the next page is slightly ambiguous melodically, but like the intermediate solo, it can be identified as Dorian because of the progression.

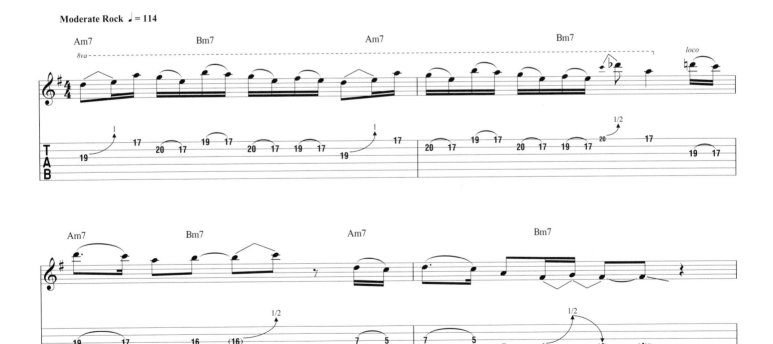

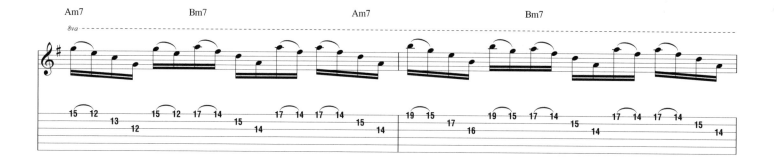

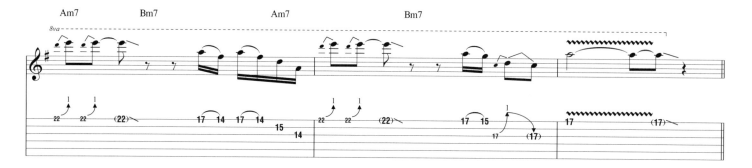

Dorian Rhythm

Let's take a look at the chords that are contained in the key of A Dorian. First we'll harmonize the scale in triads. Since A Dorian is relative to G major, it contains the same chords as the key of G major. The barre chord examples that follow are the chords demonstrated on the DVD, but we've rearranged them here into the order of the A Dorian scale.

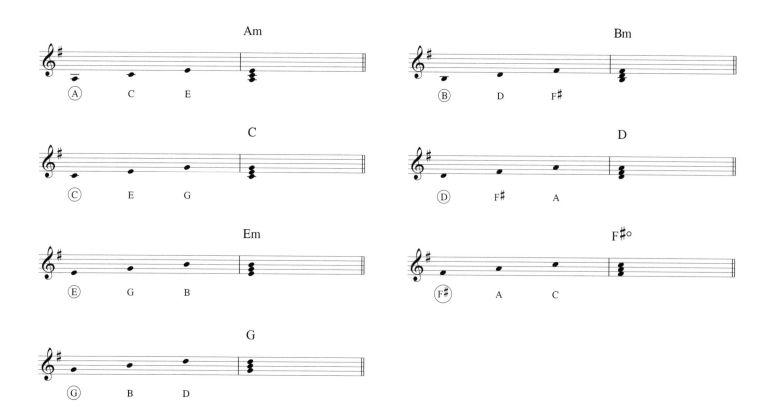

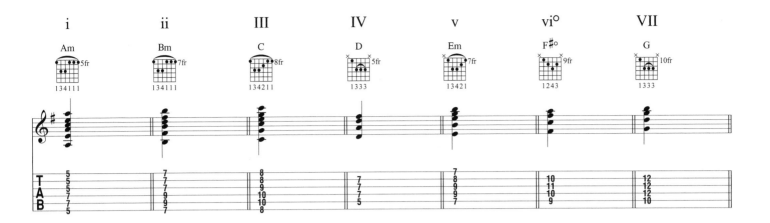

Now let's extend the chords by adding the 7ths. Some example voicings are included below. Keep in mind that these are all closed position chords and can be transposed by moving them to other positions on the fretboard.

It's important to keep in mind that, with the exception of the Ionian (major) and Aeolian (minor) keys, the functionality of these chords is quite different in modal keys. Even if you stress the Am or Am7 chord as the tonic and try to write a progression using a lot of chords in the key, it will probably end up sounding as though you're moving toward G major anyway because of the natural tendency of these chords to resolve that way. Remember that the A Dorian scale is actually an inversion of the G major scale, so playing the typically strong chords used in regular major progressions (ii, V, IV, vi) might naturally point you to G major or the relative E minor and not do much to ground you to a Dorian tonality. This is why care must be taken to emphasize the tonic of the mode without inadvertently pulling the focus towards the relative major or minor keys. The backing track used for the previous solos is shown below and is a good example of this. By using just two chords (Am7-Bm7), we've firmly established Am as the tonic. The descending riff at the end also reinforces the Am tonality.

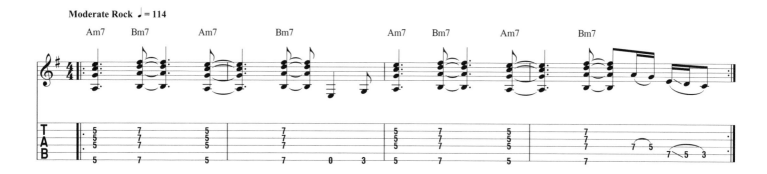

Most popular music you'll encounter won't be written in modal keys with modal key signatures. Western music will generally be shown in either a major or a minor key signature, and accidentals will be used to alter certain notes. These altered notes will give you the clues you need to help identify if a section of a song, piece, or solo is actually using a modal scale. Previously, we discussed how certain modes are major sounding and certain modes are minor sounding. The Dorian mode contains a minor 3rd, making it one of the minor sounding modes. We'll assume you're already somewhat familiar with minor scales, even though we'll cover the natural minor (Aeolian) scale in one of the upcoming chapters. For now, let's make a comparison between the A natural minor scale and the A Dorian scale.

	1	2	♭3	4	5	♭6	♭7	8
A Minor	A	B	C	D	E	F	G	A

	1	2	♭3	4	5	6	♭7	8
A Dorian	A	B	C	D	E	F♯	G	A

The only difference between the two scales is the 6th step; the minor scale uses a minor 6th (or ♭6), F, while the Dorian scale has a major 6th, F♯. Therefore, if you were to take a natural minor scale in any key and raise the 6th by a half step, it will become a Dorian scale. The scale below has been presented in the key of A minor (no sharps or flats in the key signature), but it's still a Dorian scale because we've added a sharp to the note F in the notation.

A Dorian Scale

Mastering the Modes for the Rock Guitarist

With this knowledge, you should be able to look through a piece of music and identify the mode by taking note of the accidentals. Let's take a look at the Am7-Bm7 rhythm track again, this time using an A minor key signature. The F♯'s that appear in the notation indicate that the 6th step has been raised, creating a Dorian tonality. This informs you that, although the key signature puts the song in A minor, the tonality has been altered to Dorian, making it an ideal opportunity for you to use the Dorian scales for soloing instead of the natural minor scale.

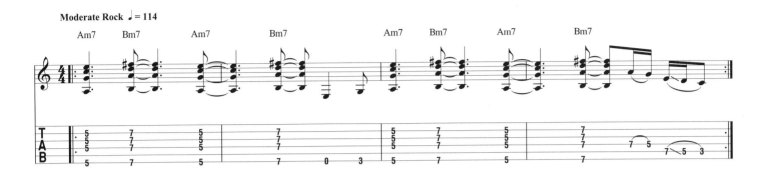

Below is the first half of the advanced solo from before, this time written in the A minor key. Notice the F♯'s in the notation and how this indicates that it's a Dorian solo.

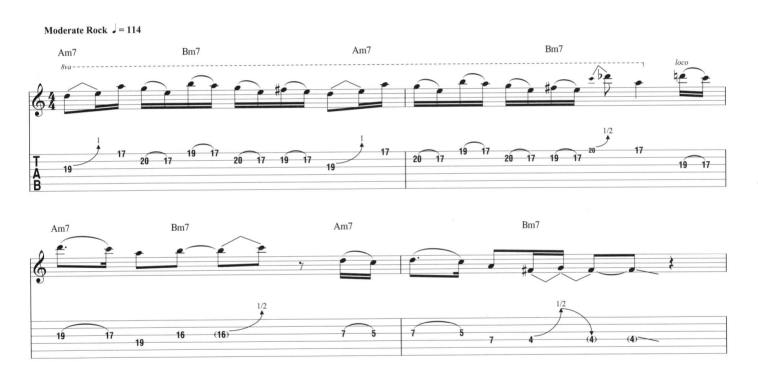

The key of E Dorian is also very common; you've probably encountered it in plenty of metal riffs that were written using an E minor key signature. The notes in E minor are E-F#-G-A-B-C-D, so the key signature for E minor contains one sharp. If we raise the 6th step, C, to a C♯ in the notation, this will give us an E Dorian tonality. The simple riff below is a good example of E Dorian.

Let's go back to our A minor and A Dorian comparison. If we look at the harmonization for both keys, you'll see that the note F# appears in quite a few of the chords in A Dorian, altering the entire tonal landscape from A minor. This makes it apparent that the chords in the Dorian key will function differently, making it difficult to establish a Dorian tonality by just using the familiar chord progressions used in natural minor keys.

Triads

A Minor	Am	B°	C	Dm	Em	F	G
A Dorian	Am	Bm	C	D	Em	F#°	G

Seventh Chords

A Minor	Am7	Bm7b5	Cmaj7	Dm7	Em7	Fmaj7	G7
A Dorian	Am7	Bm7	Cmaj7	D7	Em7	F#m7b5	Gmaj7

Although both keys have some chords in common, there are some big differences that are real game changers. In A minor, the second chord built on the note B has a flatted 5th. However, it becomes a regular Bm (or Bm7) chord in Dorian. This is why our chord progression for the Dorian rhythm track works so well. It basically stays around the Am7 tonic and alternates with the Bm7 chord, which establishes the Dorian tonality through the presence of the note F#, in effect setting it apart from the regular A minor key. Another big difference in the keys is the fourth chord that's built on D. In the minor key, it's a Dm chord. In Dorian, however, this is a D major chord (since the 3rd of the chord is now F# instead of F).

The biggest difference between minor and Dorian occurs with the root note of sixth chord—F in the minor key, and F# in the Dorian key. Many songs in minor keys are based on popular progressions that contain the VI chord. Common progressions in A minor that contain the VI chord (F) are Am-F-G-Am, Am-F-G-Em, and Am-F-C-G. In these cases, it isn't proper to use the Dorian scales for soloing, since the note F# in the A Dorian scale will constantly clash with the F major chord. However, there are many progressions written in the key of A minor that avoid the note F# altogether and instead focus around an Am or Am7 tonic. They also might contain some of the common chords C, Em, or G. These progressions give you the opportunity to solo using either the Dorian or the natural minor scale or a combination of both. Of course if the rhythm track is simply droning on an Am or Am7 continuously, you can easily play a Dorian scale over it.

Three-Octave Dorian Scales

Here are a few examples of how to combine the Dorian scale positions to play three continuous octaves. The first example uses 1st finger slides in both the ascending and descending versions. It's helpful to memorize this in terms of the finger pattern. In the ascending version, notice that on the strings that require a position change, the finger pattern is 1-2-4 after the upward slide; on the strings that have no slide (the 2nd and 4th strings), the finger pattern is also 1-2-4. While descending, the pattern is the same in reverse, with the fingering 4-2-1 before sliding down on each string to change position. Also notice the slight pivot between the 3rd and 2nd strings, where you'll need to shift your hand position by one fret.

Ascending

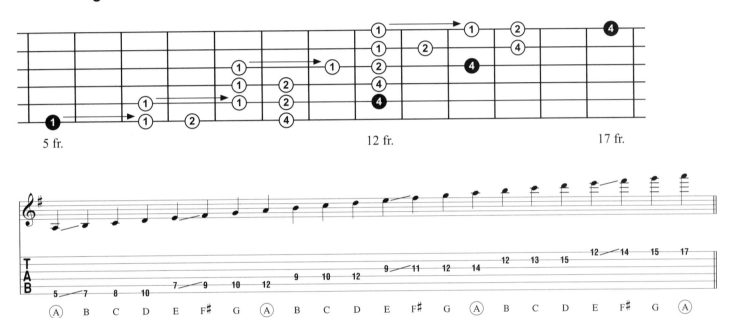

Descending

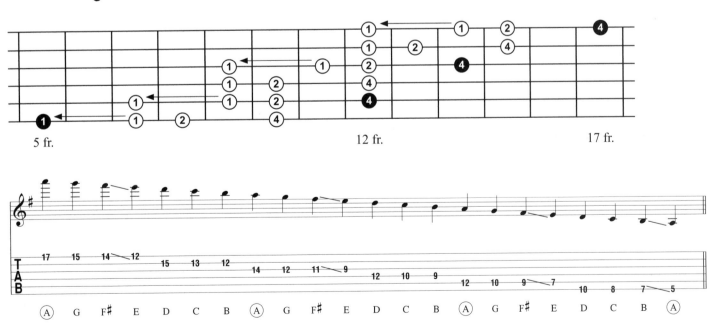

Now let's take the same notes and tab from the previous ascending example, but this time try sliding up with the 4th finger instead of the 1st. You'll notice that all of the slides occur on the strings that start with a 1-3-4 finger pattern. As before, the strings without slides use the 1-2-4 pattern.

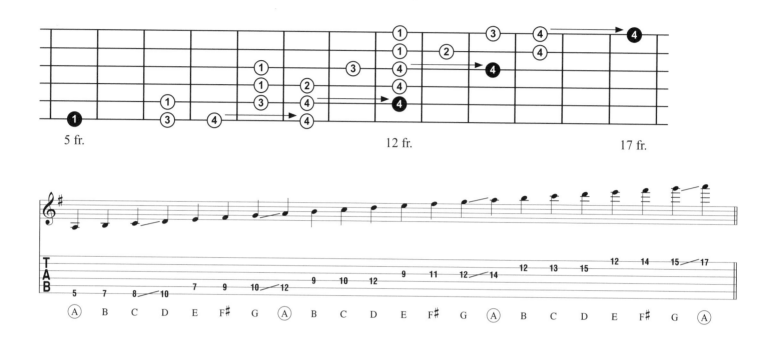

Finally, here's a way to pivot positions using the mirrored fingering technique. The finger pattern on the 4th string begins with 1-2-4 at the 4th fret and then moves up to the 9th fret to repeat the 1-2-4 pattern. The next transition occurs on the 3rd string using a 1-3-4 finger pattern.

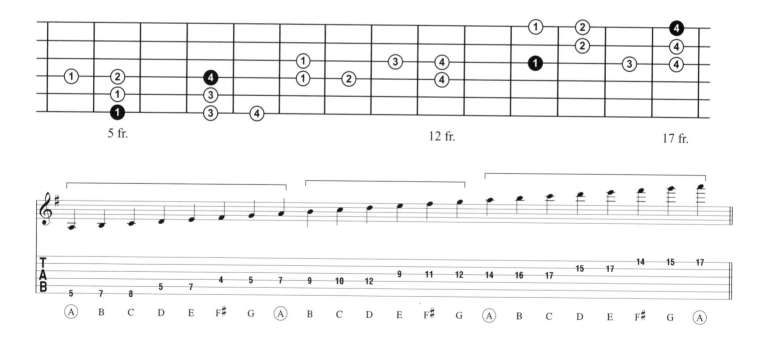

PHRYGIAN MODE

Phrygian Scale Patterns

The Phrygian mode is one of the darker minor-sounding modes. It's characterized by a flatted 2nd that many metal bands have used extensively to create ominous riffs. The E Phrygian scale can be heard in many songs by Metallica, including "Wherever I May Roam." If a song is in an E minor tonality but includes the flatted 2nd, F♮, then the E Phrygian mode is being employed.

For this chapter, we'll cover the A Phrygian scale and harmonic analysis. Since the Phrygian scale is built on the 3rd step of the major scale, and the note A is the 3rd note of the F major scale, we can determine that F major is the relative major key to A Phrygian. Therefore, A Phrygian has the same key signature as F major and contains one flat (B♭). Here are the five moveable scale patterns for A Phrygian. If you already know your minor scale positions and where the root notes are, it should be easy to memorize the Phrygian scale positions. Just remember that the 2nd step is flatted and is always located a half step (one fret) above the root note.

Phrygian Scale Pattern #1

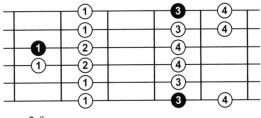

2 fr.

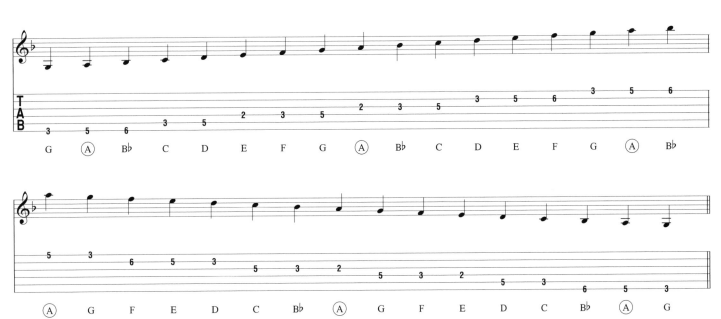

Phrygian Scale Pattern #2

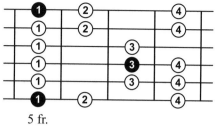

5 fr.

A Bb C D E F G A Bb C D E F G A Bb C

Bb A G F E D C Bb A G F E D C Bb A

Phrygian Scale Pattern #3

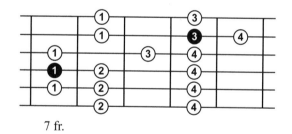

7 fr.

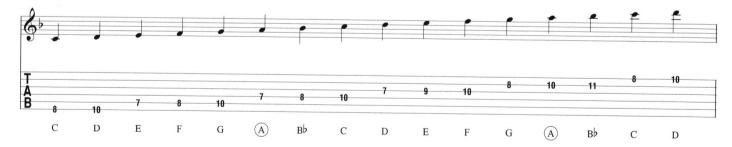

C D E F G A Bb C D E F G A Bb C D

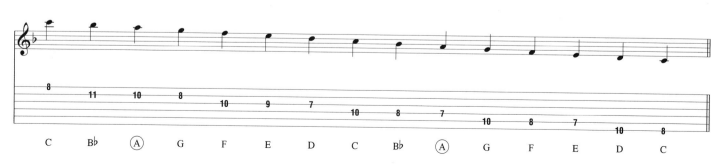

C Bb A G F E D C Bb A G F E D C

Phrygian Scale Pattern #4

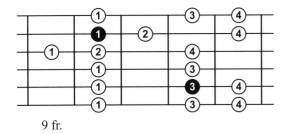

9 fr.

D E F G (A) Bb C D E F G (A) Bb C D E F

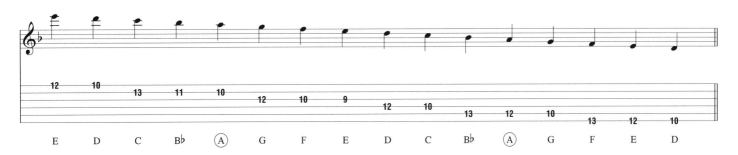

E D C Bb (A) G F E D C Bb (A) G F E D

Phrygian Scale Pattern #5

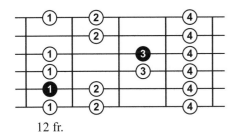

12 fr.

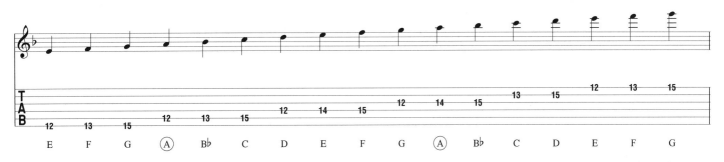

E F G (A) Bb C D E F G (A) Bb C D E F G

F E D C Bb (A) G F E D C Bb (A) G F E

Phrygian Solos

Beginner Solo

Here's a short, beginner Phrygian solo in the style of Jefferson Airplane. The flatted 2nd (Bb) is very prominent in the first measure and conveniently sets up the Phrygian tonality. The use of the triplet hammer-on and pull-off combination between the root note A and flatted 2nd is a familiar device that you'll encounter in many solos utilizing this scale.

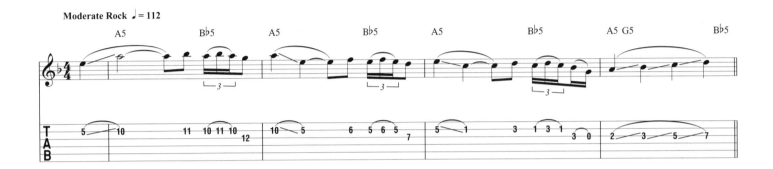

Intermediate Solo

The following intermediate solo is reminiscent of the style of Randy Rhoads. There are a few interesting bends with partial releases that characterize his style and cause the solo to momentarily drift away from the Phrygian sound. The entire solo is played in 5th position and contains a long series of hammer-on and pull-off tuplets that outline a full octave of the Phrygian scale.

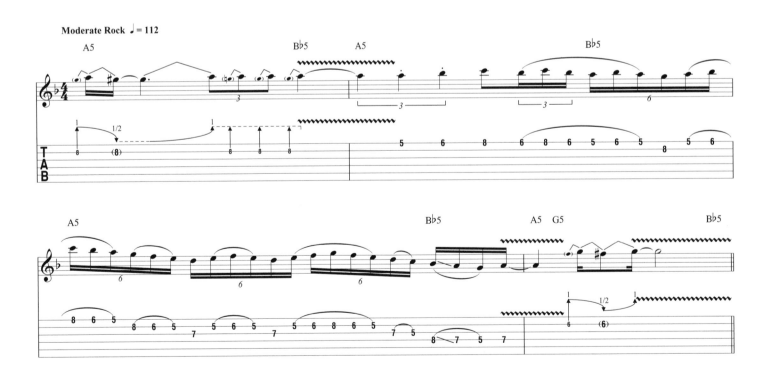

Advanced Solo

The advanced solo is something in the style of what Yngwie Malmsteen might play using the Phrygian scale. Notice that the unison bends in the 1st and 2nd measures and the 5th and 6th measures are played over a new section of the rhythm track that moves up to the F5 chord, which is also the tonic of the relative F major key. The 3rd and 4th measures contain another series of tuplet hammer-ons and pull-offs that outline the Phrygian tonality, similar to what was played in the intermediate example. The solo ends with a rapid series of right hand taps that travel up the neck.

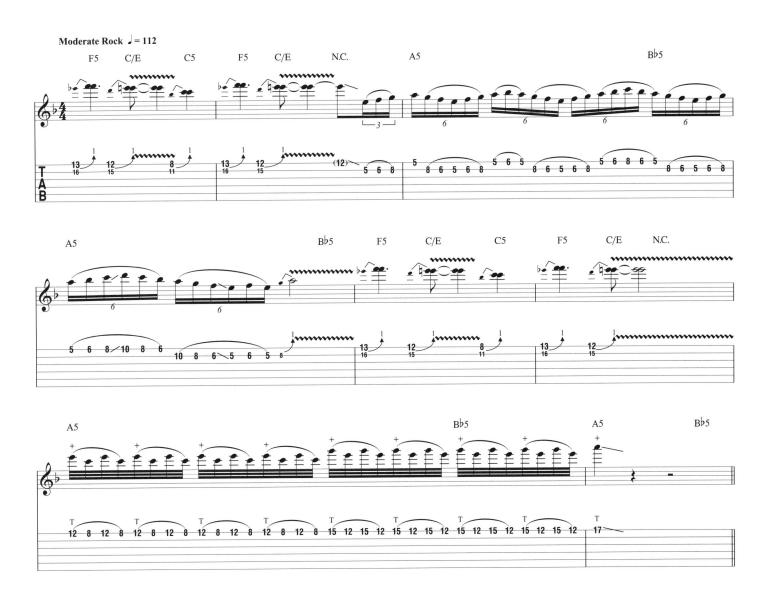

Phrygian Rhythm

Now let's harmonize the A Phrygian scale and see what chords are available in the key. First we'll show the harmonization using triads, followed by the closed position barre chords demonstrated on the DVD, which we've arranged in the order of the Phrygian scale. These are also the same chords found in the relative key of F major. Following the simple major, minor, and diminished chords, we'll harmonize the scale again adding the 7th to each chord and present some examples of how they can be voiced on the guitar. All of these chords are moveable and can be transposed to other keys. Just like with the Dorian mode, some of these chords can be problematic if you attempt to make them function the way they would in the regular major or minor keys. For example, the fifth chord is now diminished and should probably be avoided in most progressions. As you'll see when we look at the modal rhythm track, simple power chords work well to outline the Phrygian tonality.

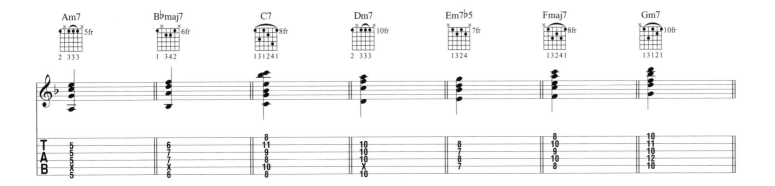

Here's the rhythm track that was played behind the previous solos. The tonic is firmly established as A by the A5 power chords, while the Phrygian tonality is established through the use of the Bb5 and G5 power chords. In the 9th measure, we modulate up to a figure using the F5, C/E, and C5 power chords just to change things up a little. The advanced solo has a section of corresponding unison bends that fits well over this part. Notice how we aren't using much more than power chords to set up and establish the key. This is a common characteristic of modal rhythms played in Phrygian.

As we discussed in the Dorian chapter, you won't commonly see Western music written in modal key signatures, but oftentimes they'll be presented in major or minor keys and utilize accidentals to alter the music into a modal tonality. The key of A Phrygian will usually appear with an A minor key signature (no sharps or flats) but will have B♭'s present in the music notation to alert you that the Phrygian mode is being implied. Below is a comparison of the intervals in the A natural minor scale and the A Phrygian scale.

	1	2	♭3	4	5	♭6	♭7	8
A Minor	A	B	C	D	E	F	G	A

	1	♭2	♭3	4	5	♭6	♭7	8
A Phrygian	A	B♭	C	D	E	F	G	A

You can see that the scales are identical except for the flatted 2nd, B♭. Take a look at the A Phrygian scale presented below in an A minor key signature—rather than the relative F major key signature—with the B♭ added in the notation.

A Phrygian Scale

Below are the first four measures of the previous Phrygian modal rhythm, written in the more common key of A minor. You can see that everything is identical except now we have lots of B♭'s on the staff to indicate that a Phrygian tonality is being used, letting you know that this is an excellent opportunity to solo using the Phrygian mode.

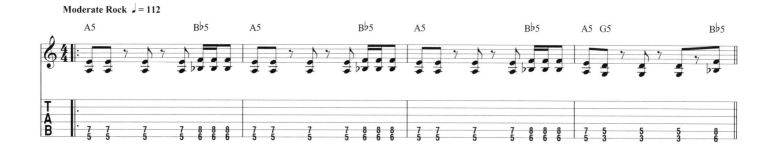

Now here's the beginner Phrygian solo shown using the A minor key signature with the B♭'s in the notation.

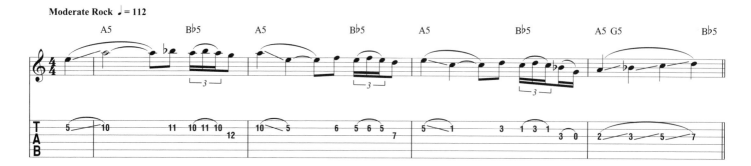

One of the most common Phrygian keys that you'll encounter is E Phrygian, used extensively by thrash metal bands like Metallica. Since E is the 3rd step of the C major scale, E Phrygian will technically have no sharps or flats in the scale and will consist of all natural notes. However, since it will usually be presented in the more common E minor key signature containing one sharp (F♯), you'll often see these songs using lot's of F♮'s in the notation. Below is a typical E Phrygian riff written in an E minor key signature.

Let's take another look at the harmonization for both the A minor and A Phrygian keys and make some comparisons so we can see what chords can be used to establish the Phrygian tonality and which should probably be avoided.

Triads

A Minor	Am	B°	C	Dm	Em	F	G
A Phrygian	Am	B♭	C	Dm	E°	F	Gm

Seventh Chords

A Minor	Am7	Bm7♭5	Cmaj7	Dm7	Em7	Fmaj7	G7
A Phrygian	Am7	B♭maj7	C7	Dm7	Em7♭5	Fmaj7	Gm7

Since the III, iv, and VI triads are the same, they won't do much to help distinguish between the minor and Phrygian keys. The B♭ chord is really the key to establishing the Phrygian sound, and in most cases, simple power chords or single note riffs centered around the A, B♭, and G notes will be most effective. It's also good to keep in mind that if you've got a rhythm part that's basically just playing the Am7 tonic, this is an ideal place to solo with the Phrygian scale. All of the notes of the minor-seventh chord are present in Phrygian, and none of the other notes in the scale will clash with it. The diminished or minor seventh flat five E chords in Phrygian usually won't be used effectively, but you may see cases where they're present and slightly altered. You'll eventually learn to carefully execute your soloing and avoid clashing with the chord tones. Most importantly, remember to firmly ground the tonic as Am or Am7 in your rhythm parts, because if you start using too many of the other chords (C7, Dm7, Fmaj7), it will undoubtedly pull the tonality back to the relative F major or D minor keys. Be aware that when we discuss the rules and theory behind these chords and their respective keys, it's to give you a basic understanding of their functionality, and all of these rules can be broken. You should always trust your ears and your instincts; if it doesn't sound like you're playing in the modal key, then it's probably because you've strayed too far from the tonic and have started emphasizing the wrong chords or scale tones.

Three-Octave Phrygian Scales

For the first three-octave Phrygian scale, try performing the slides with your 4th finger in both the ascending and descending examples as shown below. There are no difficult stretches here, but be aware of the slight position shift when moving between the 3rd and 2nd strings. You can also try to slightly rearrange the fingering on the 5th and 3rd strings in order to slide with your 1st finger.

Ascending

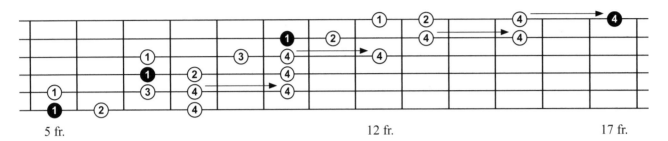

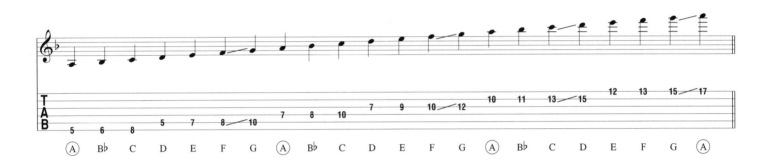

Descending

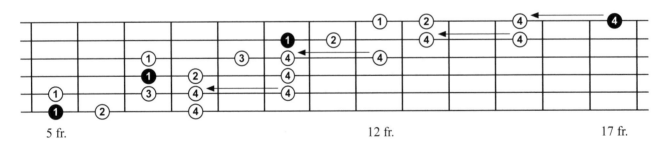

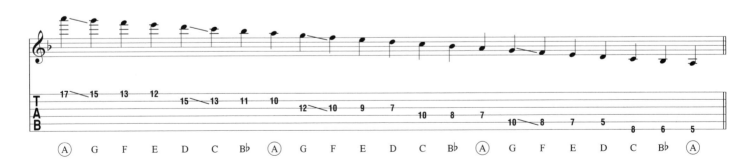

For this next example, we've used shorter half-step slides with the 1st finger and spread the notes out to perform wider stretches using a 1-2-4 fingering on every string.

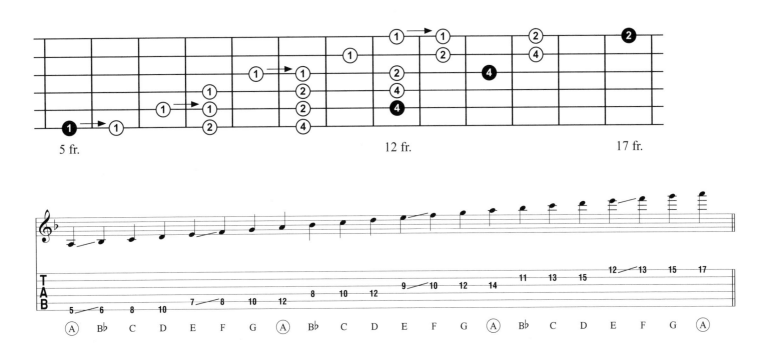

Our last example uses the mirrored fingering technique to spread the scale out into larger chunks. On the 5th string, the 1-3-4 fingering is mirrored after the position change; then on the 3rd string, the 1-2-4 fingering is mirrored.

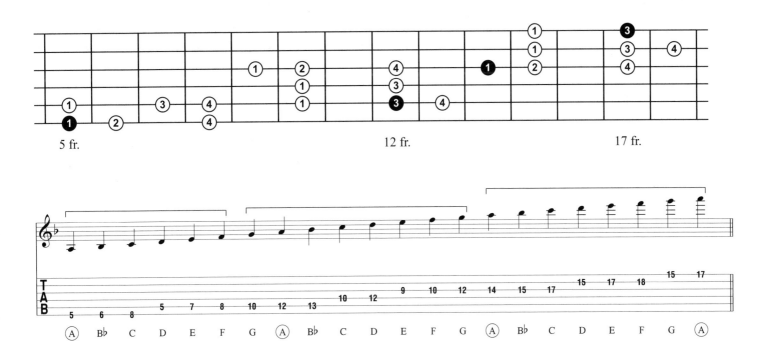

LYDIAN MODE

Lydian Scale Patterns

The Lydian mode is a major-sounding mode, characterized by the sharped (augmented) 4th, which creates tension by acting as a tritone and can also be utilized as a leading tone to the 5th. Steve Vai has used the Lydian mode extensively, most notably on the album *Passion and Warfare*. Joe Satriani also makes great use of the Lydian mode in songs such as "Flying in a Blue Dream." The beginning of the melody to *The Simpsons* theme song is another great example of the Lydian mode. The Lydian scale has a dreamy and airy quality, making it ideal to use over major seventh chords.

Since the note A is the fourth step of the E major scale, the A Lydian mode contains the same notes as E major: A-B-C#-D#-E-F#-G#-A. The augmented 4th in A Lydian is the note D#, the only note that differentiates A Lydian from the regular A major scale. Here are the five scale patterns for A Lydian on the guitar, beginning in 1st position.

Lydian Scale Pattern #1

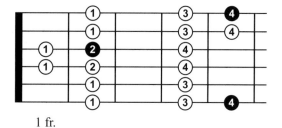

1 fr.

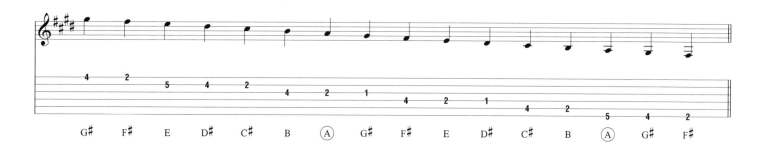

Lydian Scale Pattern #2

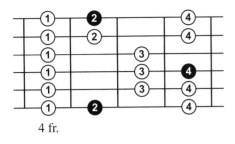

4 fr.

G# (A) B C# D# E F# G# (A) B C# D# E F# G# (A) B

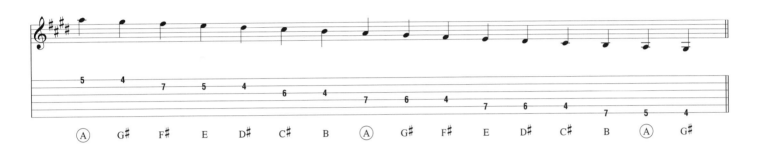

(A) G# F# E D# C# B (A) G# F# E D# C# B (A) G#

Lydian Scale Pattern #3

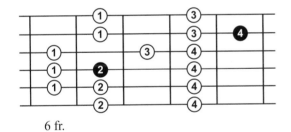

6 fr.

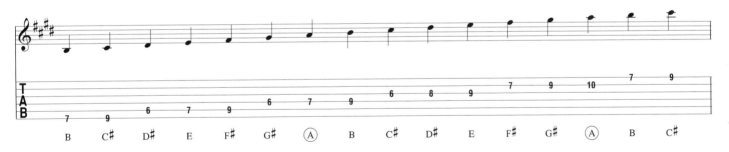

B C# D# E F# G# (A) B C# D# E F# G# (A) B C#

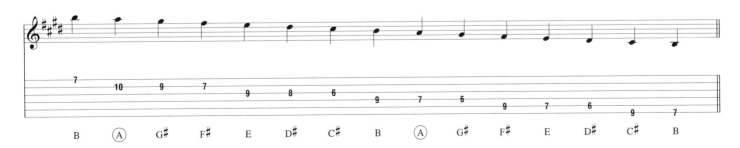

B (A) G# F# E D# C# B (A) G# F# E D# C# B

Lydian Scale Pattern #4

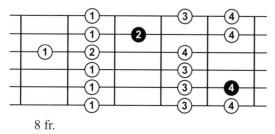

8 fr.

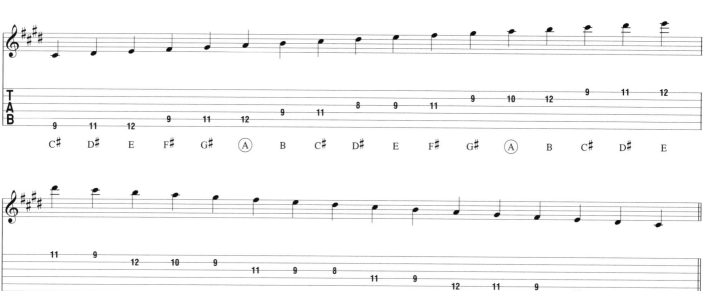

Lydian Scale Pattern #5

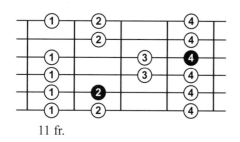

11 fr.

Lydian Solos

Beginner Solo

Our first Lydian solo is in the style of Alex Lifeson from Rush. The beginning phrase of the solo ends with two bends up to the D♯—the augmented 4th—establishing the Lydian sound right away. The next phrase is a series of triplet hammer-on and pull-off slides that also showcase the D♯ and help to establish the major sound by ending on a bend up to the note C♯—the major 3rd of the scale. The intro phrase is then repeated, this time transposed a 3rd higher on the fretboard, leading into a tasteful run that again ends on a bend up to the major 3rd. Follow along with the DVD to see the lead broken down by section.

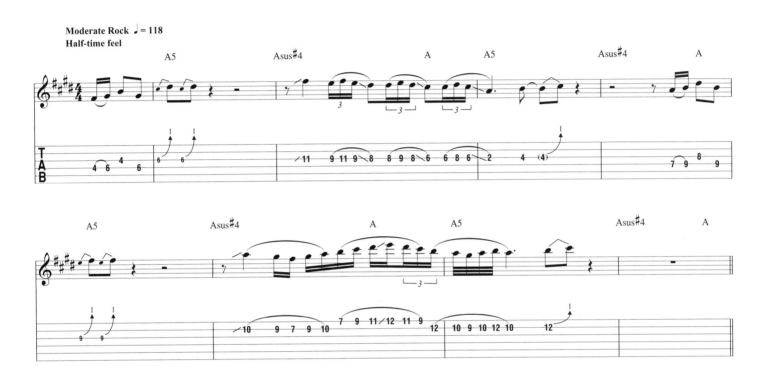

Intermediate Solo

The following intermediate solo is in the style of John Petrucci from the band Dream Theater. Notice how the intro lick starts out sounding like a simple major pentatonic scale, but then it moves into a pivoting phrase that showcases the D♯ and brings in the more interesting Lydian sound. The 4th measure follows with a descending lick that pivots between notes on the 1st string and legato slides on the 2nd string. The whole scale is being used so there's no shortage of the major 3rd, augmented 4th, and major 7th intervals necessary to establish the Lydian tonality.

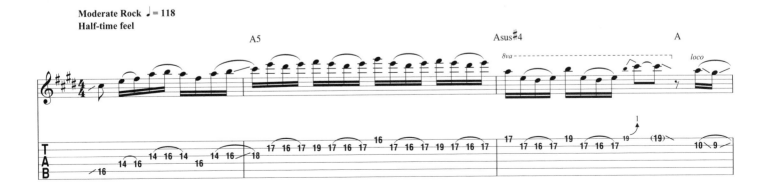

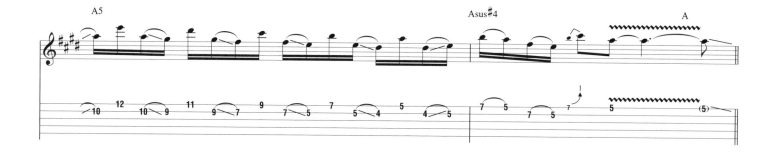

Advanced Solo

The advanced solo is a series of right-hand taps and pull-offs in the style of Joe Satriani. It starts out with both hands descending down the neck in a quick series of tapped tuplets, with the left hand settling in at around the 5th position. From there, the right hand gradually works its way back up the neck while alternating tapped phrases on the 1st and 2nd strings. The solo finishes off with a tapped bend and release on the first string—tap the note at the 14th fret while bending up the string with the left hand at the 7th fret, then release the right-hand tap while holding the left-hand bend. This is a complicated solo, so start out practicing slowly, then gradually build up speed.

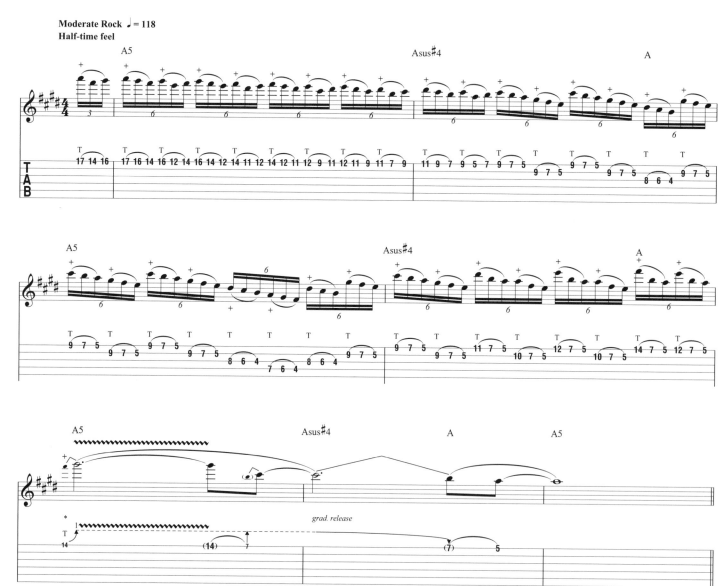

*Tap and hold note with right hand while bending up with 3rd finger of left hand at 7th fret, then pull off to left hand note and gradually release bend.

Mastering the Modes for the Rock Guitarist

Lydian Rhythm

Here are the triads in A Lydian, followed by the example guitar chords that were presented on the DVD. These are the same chords that are used in the relative key of E major, but we've again rearranged the order of the chords to the key of A Lydian. It's easy to see how the chords that contain the sharped 4th (D♯) of the scale differ from the chords in a regular A major key, causing the II, iv°, and vii chords to function differently.

Now let's add the 7th to these chords and take a look at some example voicings on the guitar. One of the main differences between the A Lydian and A major keys is the 4th chord, which in a regular major key would be a Dmaj7 chord. But since we've moved the root note of the chord up by a half step for Lydian, it becomes a D♯m7♭5 chord.

The following Lydian modal rhythm that was used for soloing on the DVD stays around the tonic A major chord throughout. The open A major chord is arpeggiated by picking the notes out individually, while a melody is incorporated on the 2nd string that brings in the ♯4 (D♯) to establish the Lydian tonality. The second half of the progression briefly utilizes the B major chord, which also contains a D♯ and helps to reinforce the Lydian sound. You can see from the chord analysis above the music how the 2nd string melody creates the implied A5 to Asus♯4 to A progression. The philosophy behind this progression is similar to the Dorian rhythm track from the previous chapter; both rhythms primarily drone on the tonic chord and introduce just the key pitches that reinforce the modal tonality.

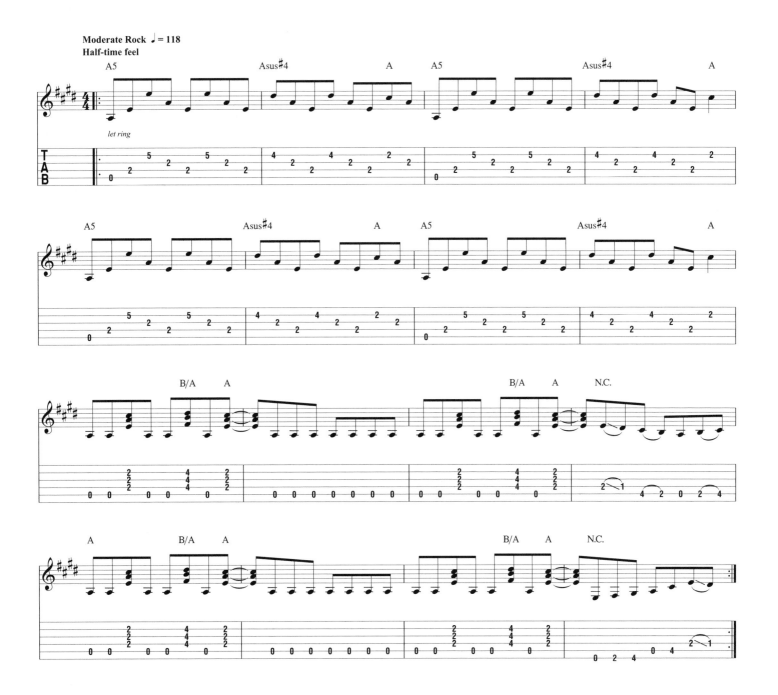

Below is a comparison chart of the notes and intervals in the A major (Ionian) scale and the A Lydian scale, showing that they're identical except for the 4th step, D♯. If you've got the Ionian mode scales down, then all you need to do is sharp the 4th, and that will give you the Lydian mode.

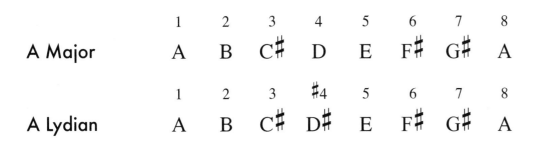

	1	2	3	4	5	6	7	8
A Major	A	B	C♯	D	E	F♯	G♯	A

	1	2	3	♯4	5	6	7	8
A Lydian	A	B	C♯	D♯	E	F♯	G♯	A

Here's the Lydian scale written out in the key of A major with three sharps in the key signature. A sharp has been added in the notation to augment the fourth step.

A Lydian Scale

Below are the first four measures of the Lydian rhythm track, also written out in A major. When you see a piece of music in A major with D♯'s present in the notation, it's a good indication that the piece is in the Lydian mode.

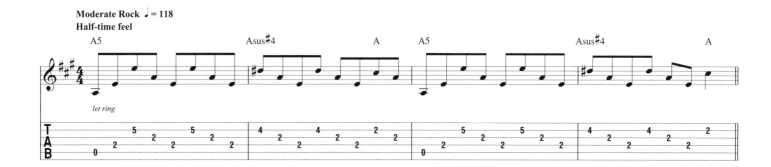

Now let's take a look at a comparison chart for the triads and seventh chords for A major and A Lydian. Notably, the second chord in the key has changed from B minor to B major. This makes the B chord an ideal candidate to use in an A Lydian progression to distinguish it from the regular major tonality. The B chord was used in the Lydian rhythm track as well.

Triads

A Major	A	Bm	C♯m	D	E	F♯m	G♯°
A Lydian	A	B	C♯m	D♯°	E	F♯m	G♯m

Seventh Chords

A Major	Amaj7	Bm7	C♯m7	Dmaj7	E7	F♯m7	G♯m7♭5
A Lydian	Amaj7	B7	C♯m7	D♯m7♭5	Emaj7	F♯m7	G♯m7

Three-Octave Lydian Scales

The Lydian pattern below covers three octaves of the scale by using 1st-finger ascending and descending slides. After the wide 1-2-4 fingering stretch on the 6th string, the finger pattern follows a consistent 1-3-4 pattern that you slide into with your first finger on the 5th, 4th, and 2nd strings.

Ascending

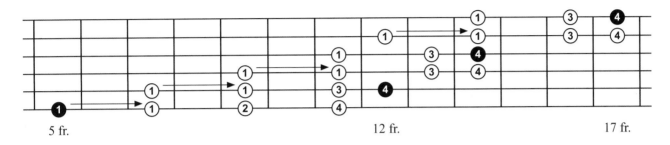

Descending

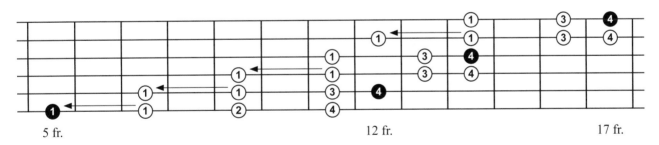

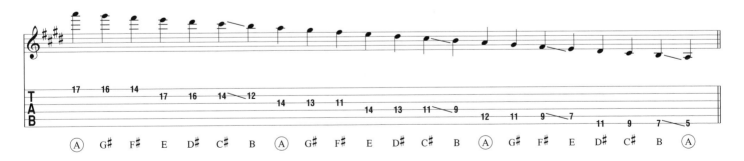

For the second version of the three-octave Lydian scale, we're using 1st-finger slides again but keeping the 1-2-4 finger stretch consistent throughout until the 1st string, where it slides into the 1-3-4 finger pattern. You can also alter the 1st-string pattern by playing the 1-2-4 fingering first and then sliding up to the high A with your 4th finger.

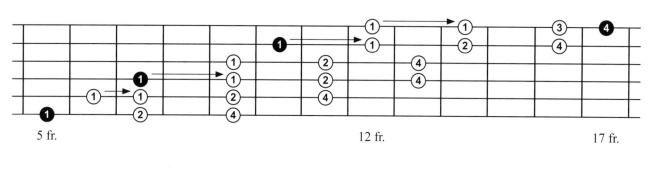

Finally, here's a version of the three-octave Lydian scale using the mirrored fingering technique. It uses a 1-3-4 fingering to shift positions on the 5th string and a 1-2-4 fingering to shift positions on the 3rd string.

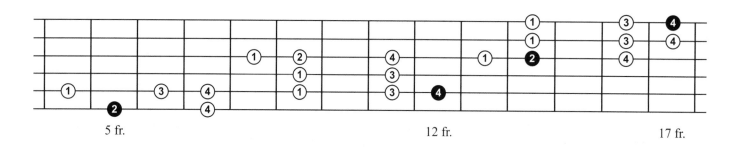

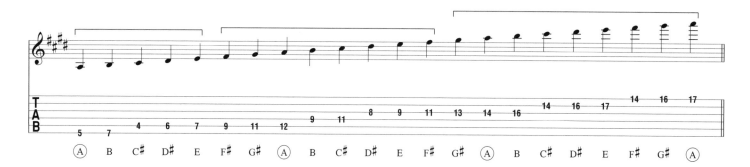

MIXOLYDIAN MODE

Mixolydian Scale Patterns

As with the Lydian mode, the Mixolydian mode differs from the major scale by only one note. Mixoydian contains a flatted 7th, making it ideal to use for soloing over dominant seventh chords. Mixolydian is one of the most popular modes, used extensively in rock, classic rock, and blues. Some famous examples are "L.A. Woman" by the Doors, "Norwegian Wood (This Bird Has Flown)" by the Beatles, and "Sweet Child O' Mine" by Guns 'N' Roses.

Mixolydian is built on the fifth step of the major scale. Since the note A is the fifth step of the D major scale, the A Mixolydian scale will contain the same notes as D major: A-B-C#-D-E-F#-G-A. The following five scale patterns show the Mixolydian scale on the guitar, starting with the first pattern in 2nd position on the fretboard.

Mixolydian Scale Pattern #1

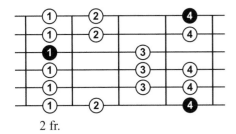

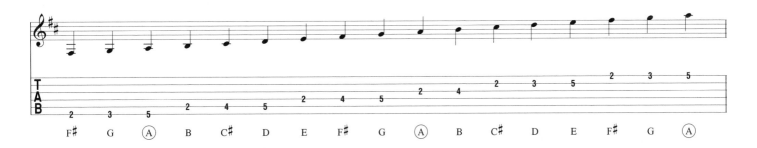

Mixolydian Scale Pattern #2

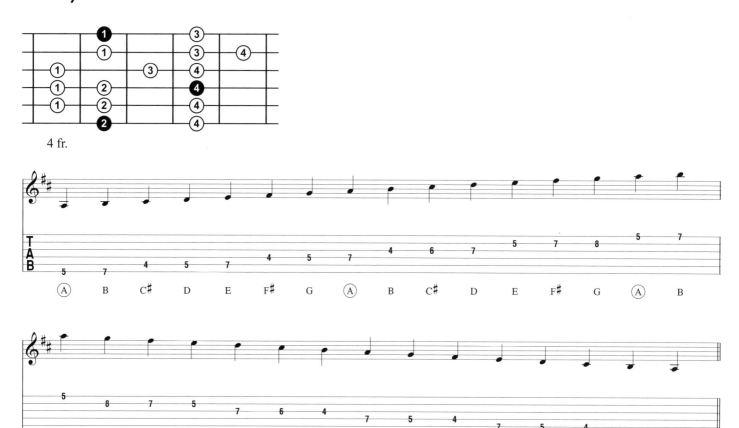

4 fr.

Mixolydian Scale Pattern #3

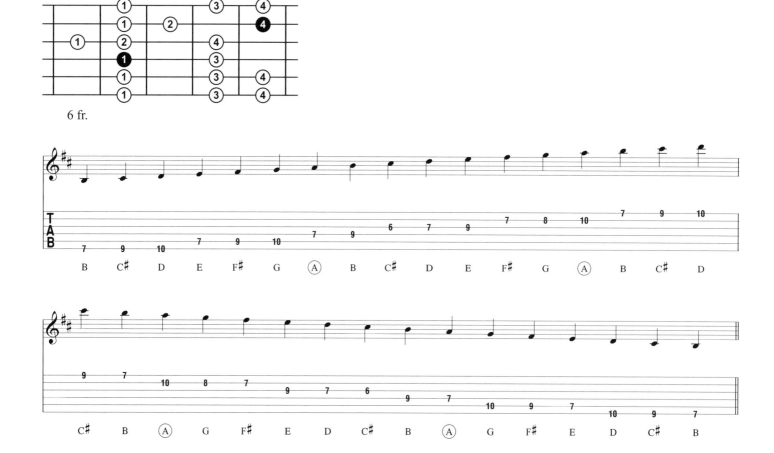

6 fr.

Mixolydian Scale Pattern #4

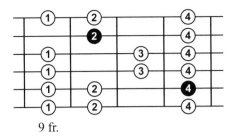

9 fr.

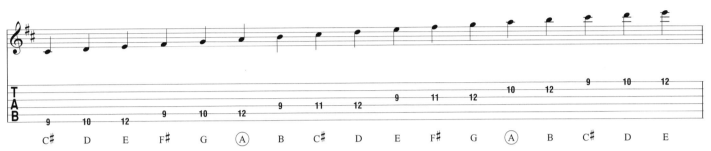

C♯　D　E　F♯　G　Ⓐ　B　C♯　D　E　F♯　G　Ⓐ　B　C♯　D　E

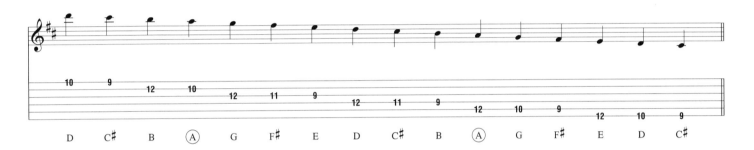

D　C♯　B　Ⓐ　G　F♯　E　D　C♯　B　Ⓐ　G　F♯　E　D　C♯

Mixolydian Scale Pattern #5

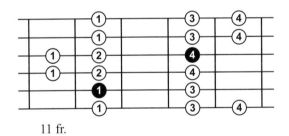

11 fr.

E　F♯　G　Ⓐ　B　C♯　D　E　F♯　G　Ⓐ　B　C♯　D　E　F♯　G

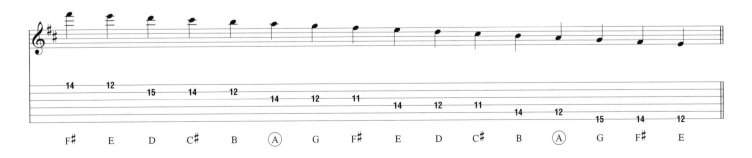

F♯　E　D　C♯　B　Ⓐ　G　F♯　E　D　C♯　B　Ⓐ　G　F♯　E

Mixolydian Solos

Beginner Solo

The beginner Mixolydian solo is in the style of Eric Clapton. The intro riff and subsequent bends up to G outline the notes from an A7 chord and help to establish the Mixolydian tonality right away. Notice how the rhythm track is based on the I, IV, and V chords from the relative D major key, but they are arranged in a way that emphasizes A as the tonic.

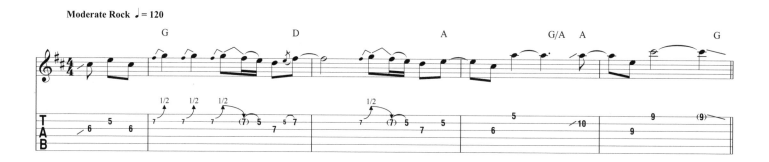

Intermediate Solo

The intermediate solo is something along the lines of what Slash from Guns 'N' Roses might play. This is actually more closely related to a simple A major pentatonic scale since it doesn't contain the ♭7th (G) at all, but since the chord progression outlines the Mixolydian mode, it works fine.

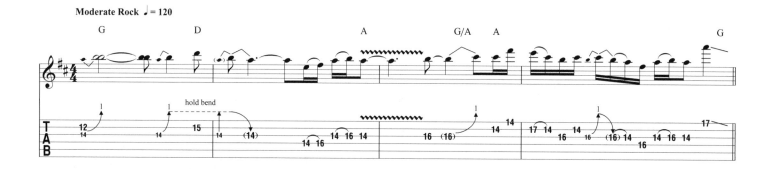

Advanced Solo

Here's another solo in the style of Joe Satriani. The first half contains a tasteful series of descending arpeggios that handily outline each of the chords in the progression. The riff that begins with the bends in measure 5 emphasizes the third of each chord, with the B being showcased for the G chord, the F♯ emphasized on the D chord, and ending on the C♯ when the progression changes to the A chord. The final two measures of the solo finishes it up with a nice A major pentatonic pull-off run.

Mixolydian Rhythm

Here's the harmonization for the key of A Mixolydian, which contains the same chords as the relative key of D major. The triads are shown below, followed by the guitar chords from the DVD placed in the order of the Mixolydian scale.

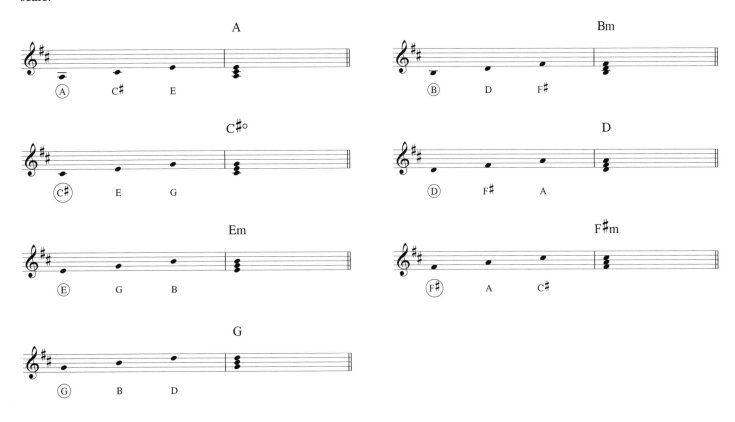

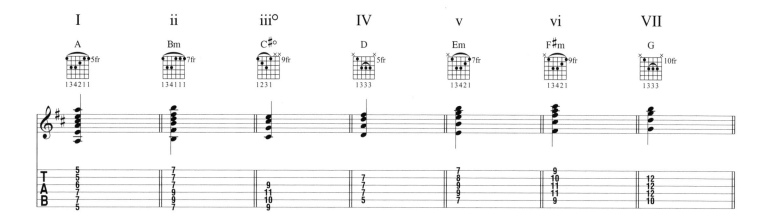

Looking at the chords above, you can see that the Mixolydian harmonization does have a lot in common with the regular major scale harmonization. This is why we can use some typical progressions for Mixolydian progressions that may not work as easily in other modes. Below we've added the 7th to the chords and shown some example chords for guitar. Notice that the tonic chord A becomes a dominant seventh. The Mixolydian scale is an excellent candidate for soloing over dominant chords. You'll find that many blues progressions use dominant seventh chords throughout, and in instances like these, you can play Mixolydian scales throughout that correspond to each of the chords.

Here's the Mixolydian rhythm that we played the previous solos over. As we mentioned before, the G, D, and A chords are the corresponding IV, I, and V chords from the relative key of D major, but we're emphasizing the A chord as the tonic here. This is done not only with the order of the chords, but also by pedaling the open A note under the changes throughout.

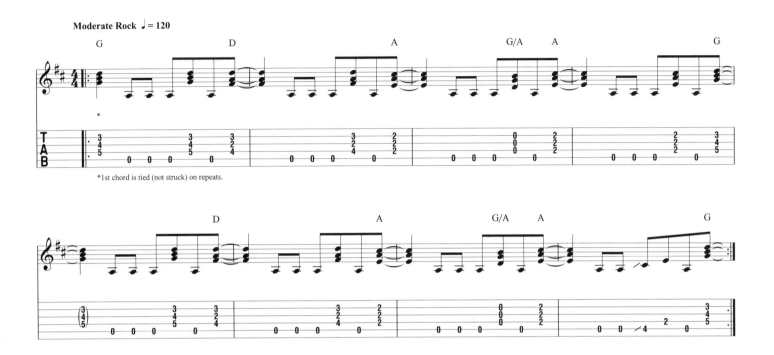

*1st chord is tied (not struck) on repeats.

Let's take a look at the comparison between the dominant sounding A Mixolydian scale and the A major scale; you can see below that the only difference is the ♭7th (G). You'll frequently encounter songs written in A major that employ an A Mixolydian tonality, easily identified by the G♮'s that appear in the notation. Below the chart is the A Mixolydian scale written out using the key signature of A major, with the G♮ indicated on the staff.

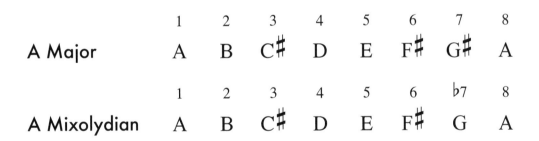

	1	2	3	4	5	6	7	8
A Major	A	B	C♯	D	E	F♯	G♯	A

	1	2	3	4	5	6	♭7	8
A Mixolydian	A	B	C♯	D	E	F♯	G	A

A Mixolydian Scale

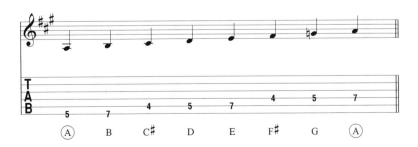

Here's the first half of the Mixolydian rhythm notated in the key of A major with the G♮'s added in the music.

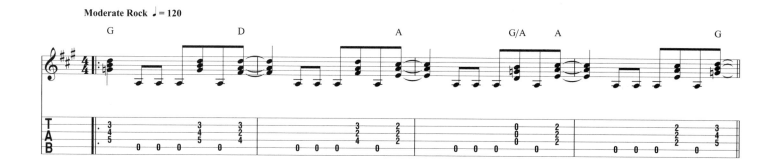

No let's take a look at the beginner solo again, this time written out in A major. The naturals have been place on the G bends in the notation.

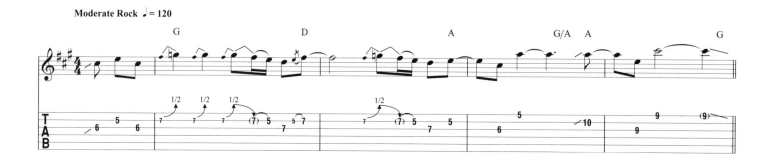

Finally, let's compare the major and Mixolydian harmonizations for the triads and seventh chords. Some of the important chords remain the same between keys, with the big exception being the fifth chord, which has switched from major to minor. You can see from this analysis how the Mixolydian is a fairly close match to the major key, making it a popular choice for soloing.

Triads

A Major	A	Bm	C♯m	D	E	F♯m	G♯°
A Mixolydian	A	Bm	C♯°	D	Em	F♯m	G

Seventh Chords

A Major	Amaj7	Bm7	C♯m7	Dmaj7	E7	F♯m7	G♯m7♭5
A Mixolydian	A7	Bm7	C♯m7♭5	Dmaj7	Em7	F♯m7	Gmaj7

Three-Octave Mixolydian Scales

The following three-octave Mixolydian scale uses 1st-finger slides and mostly follows a 1-3-4 finger pattern until the 1st string, which slides into a 1-2-4 pattern. The fingering on the 1st string can also be rearranged to follow the 1-3-4 pattern followed by a 4th-finger slide up to the high A at the 17th fret.

Ascending

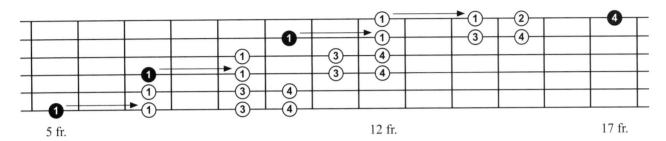

Descending

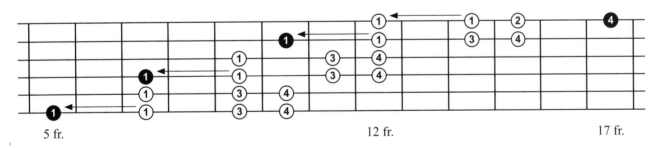

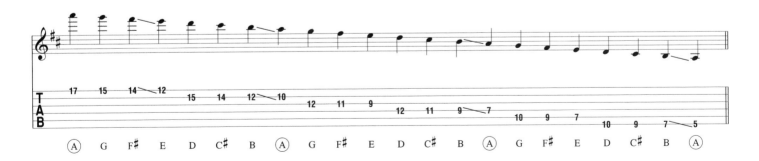

The next version of the three-octave scale uses 4th-finger slides and employs the wider 1-2-4 finger stretches on the 6th, 5th, and 4th strings.

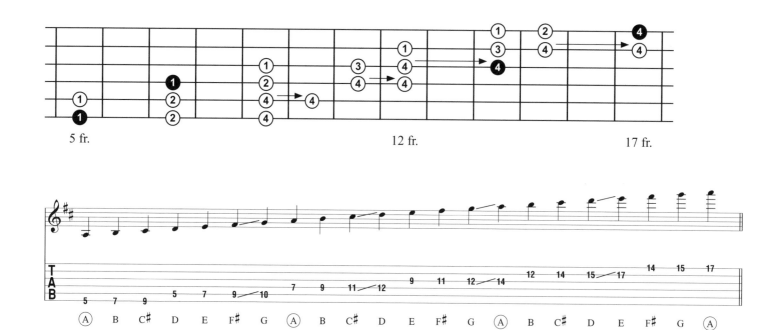

The mirrored fingering technique shown below uses a 1-2-4 fingering on the 5th string to shift positions and then a 1-3-4 fingering on the 4th string to shift positions again. This gets you up to the 14th position for one and a half octaves of the scale.

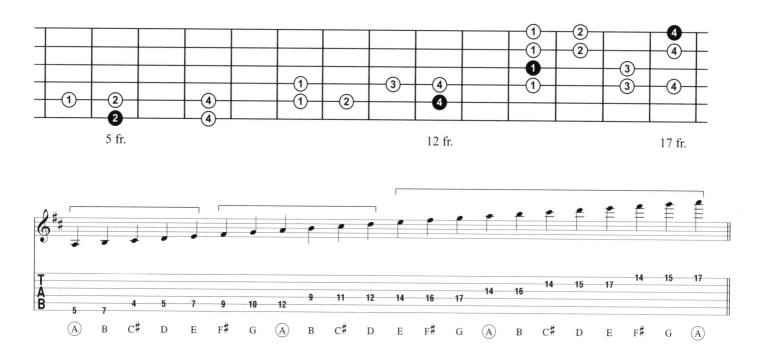

AEOLIAN MODE

Aeolian Scale Patterns

Just as the Ionian mode is the same as the major scale, the Aeolian mode is the same as the natural minor scale. You may already know your minor scales, and if you do, this is a good review that will cover the scale positions, some solo examples, harmonization, and three-octave scales. As we've shown in previous chapters, each of the modes has certain characteristic notes that define its tonality. We can call the Aeolian mode a minor-sounding scale, and what really sets it apart from other minor-sounding scales are the minor 6th and major 2nd intervals. The presence of these two intervals within the scale distinguishes Aeolian from the Dorian scale (which contains a major 6th) and the Phrygian (which contains a minor 2nd).

The key of A Aeolian (or simply referred to as A minor) contains no sharps or flats. Since Aeolian is built on the sixth step of the major scale, and A is the 6th step of C major, then A minor (Aeolian) is the relative minor scale to C major. The following are the five scale positions for A Aeolian, starting in 2nd position on the fretboard.

Aeolian Scale Pattern #1

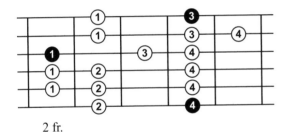

2 fr.

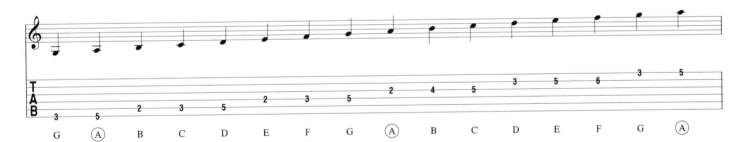

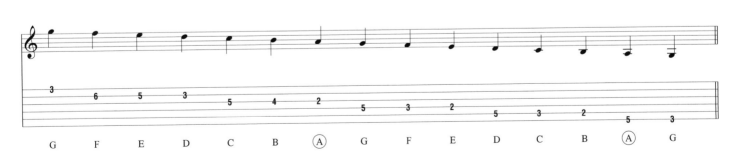

Aeolian Scale Pattern #2

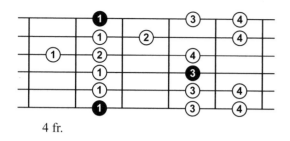

4 fr.

A B C D E F G Ⓐ B C D E F G Ⓐ B C

B Ⓐ G F E D C B Ⓐ G F E D C B Ⓐ

Aeolian Scale Pattern #3

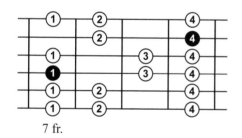

7 fr.

B C D E F G Ⓐ B C D E F G Ⓐ B C D

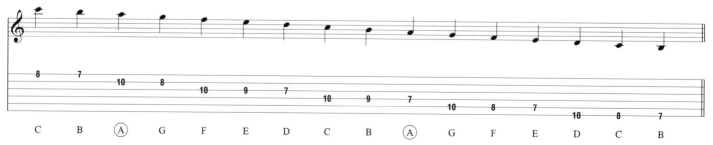

C B Ⓐ G F E D C B Ⓐ G F E D C B

Aeolian Scale Pattern #4

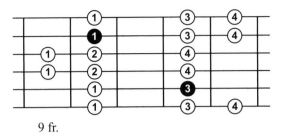

9 fr.

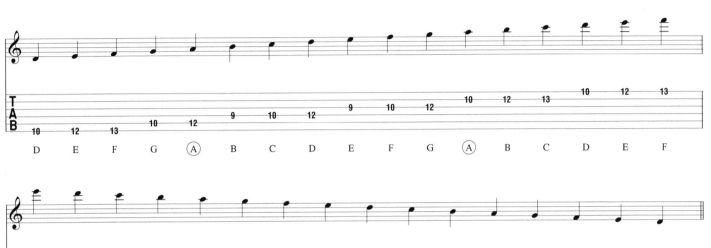

D E F G (A) B C D E F G (A) B C D E F

E D C B (A) G F E D C B (A) G F E D

Aeolian Scale Pattern #5

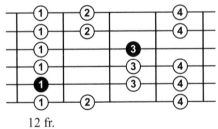

12 fr.

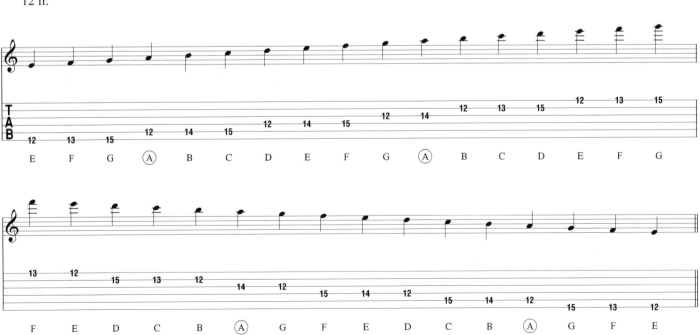

E F G (A) B C D E F G (A) B C D E F G

F E D C B (A) G F E D C B (A) G F E

Aeolian Solos

Beginner Solo

The beginning solo is a minor solo in the style of Eric Clapton. The first part of the solo is built off a simple 1st position A minor pentatonic scale at the 5th fret. The second part of the solo introduces the minor 6th scale tone F, fittingly over the F major chord in the progression.

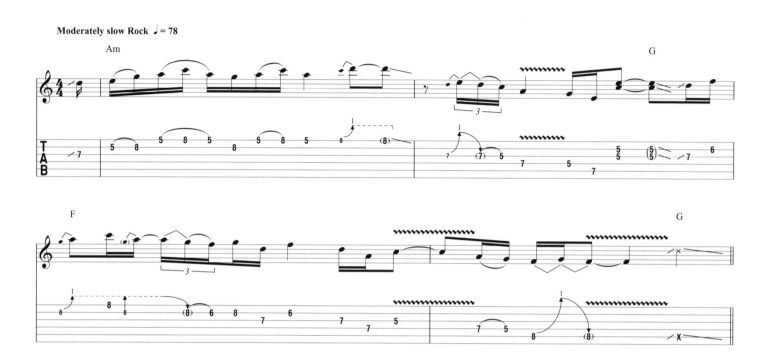

Intermediate Solo

This next solo will be something in the style of Jimmy Page from Led Zeppelin. We're again starting out with the 1st position Am pentatonic scale as our foundation, with the 2nd scale tone B introduced at the end of the 1st measure. The minor 6th F is then introduced again when the progression gets to the F major chord. The solo finishes up by moving up to the next position and playing a series of pull-offs using what's known as the extended box position.

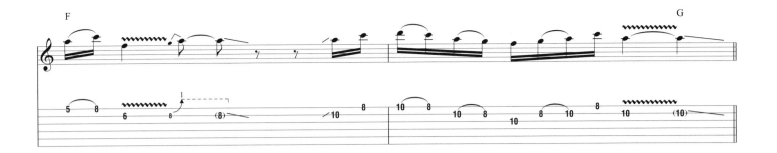

Advanced Solo

The advanced solo is played in the style of Randy Rhoads. Notice that the progression has modulated up to the iv chord, Dm, for this section. The N.C. that follows in the 3rd measure has an Em tonality implied by the bass, and we can see that the scale positions being used have moved up to around the 10th fret for the Dm chord and then up to the 12th fret area (Em) to finish off the solo. We are still using the notes in A Aeolian, but it can arguably be said that we've also modulated the scale to the relative modes of the A Aeolian to fit the chord progression. This is a popular technique that you'll encounter quite often. Once you've got all of your modal scales down and you encounter progressions that hang on a single chord for a few measures at a time, you'll be able to fittingly apply a different modal scale to each of the chords, rather than playing one continuous mode for an entire solo.

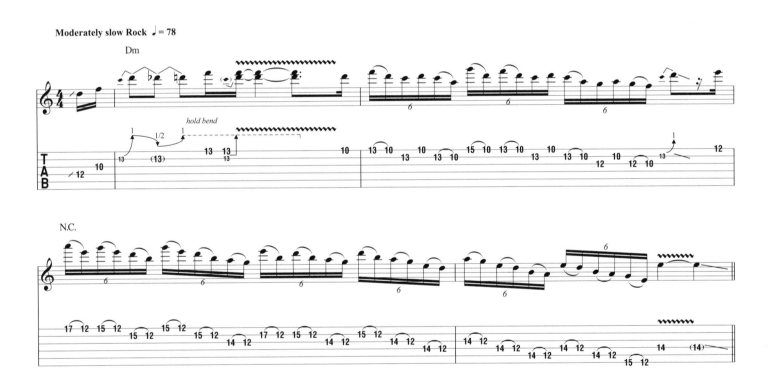

Aeolian Rhythm

Let's harmonize the A Aeolian scale and see what chords are available for creating rhythms in this key. We'll begin with the major, minor, and diminished triads, followed by the barre chords demonstrated on the DVD, but placed in the order of the Aeolian key. Like the Ionian (major) keys, the chords in Aeolian (minor) keys function well together and lend themselves to just as many familiar progressions.

Since the chords in this key are very useful in writing progressions, let's take a look at some more common voicings for the triads on the guitar. Some of these chords are in open position, but the ones that aren't can be transposed and moved to other keys.

Mastering the Modes for the Rock Guitarist

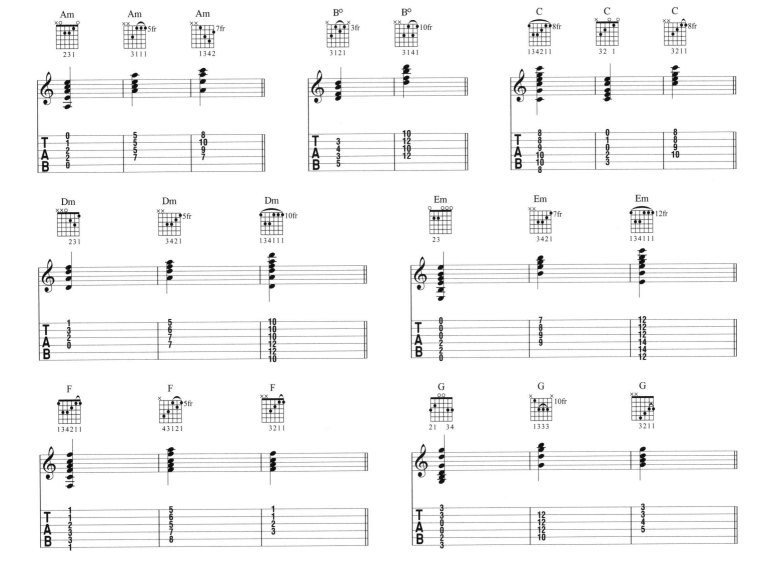

Now let's follow through and add the 7ths above the triads to create the seventh chords in A Aeolian. Example voicings for these chords are are presented after the harmonization below.

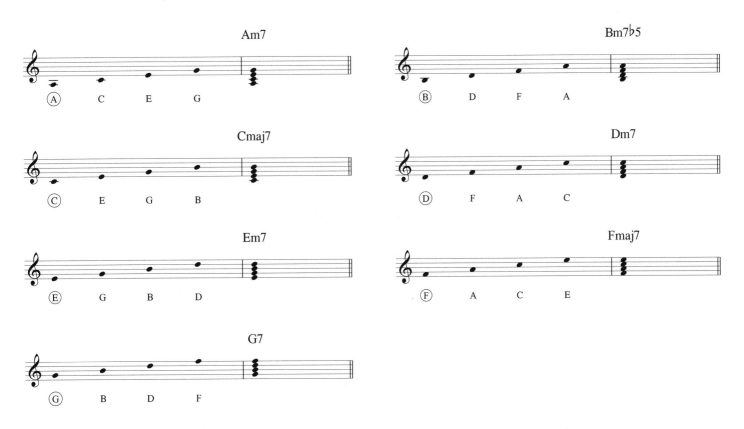

Here's the Aeolian rhythm track featured on the DVD. The first eight measures are a standard Am-G-F chord progression using basic barre chords. The progression then moves up to the Dm chord (iv chord) and finishes up with an E minor pentatonic single note riff that implies the minor v chord, Em.

Moderate Rock ♩ = 130

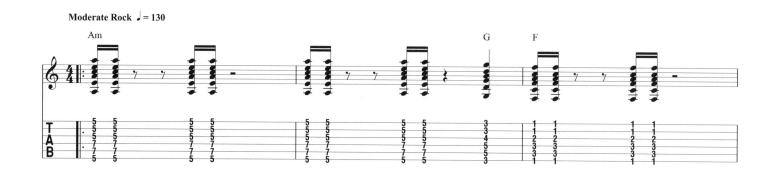

As we mentioned before, the last four measures can be used to imply other modal scales as well. Since A Aeolian is the relative minor to C major, let's determine what modes are relative to the Dm and N.C.(Em) chords. Since D is the second step of the C major scale, then a D Dorian scale fits well here too. Since E is the third step of the scale, you can probably get away with trying out an E Phrygian scale against the last two measures. The more you experiment, the more you'll see what works or doesn't. These rules exist to be learned and then bent or broken, but knowing the theory will help you to avoid playing pitches that clash with the chords or the key. For example, you want to avoid playing a major-sounding scale against a minor-sounding chord and vice versa.

Three-Octave Aeolian Scales

The first in this series of three-octave Aeolian scales uses 4th-finger slides ascending and descending. The 1-3-4 finger pattern is used consistently until we reach the 1st string, where a 1-2-4 pattern is necessary. Notice that if you were to slide up with the 1st finger instead on the 6th through 2nd strings, you would change the stationary part of the pattern to 1-2-4 on those strings as well.

Ascending

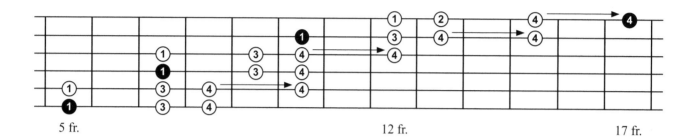

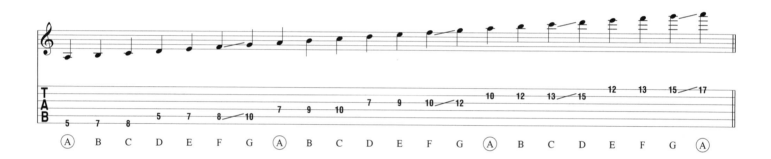

Descending

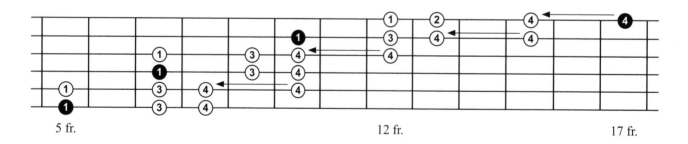

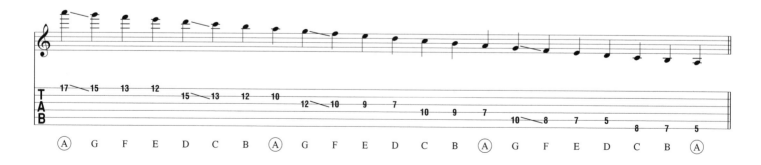

Mastering the Modes for the Rock Guitarist

Our second version of the three-octave scale utilizes 1st-finger slides throughout. With the exception of the fingering on the 6th string, the rest of the scale pattern uses the wide 1-2-4 finger stretches that are useful for symetrical hammer-on and pull-off riffs on adjacent strings.

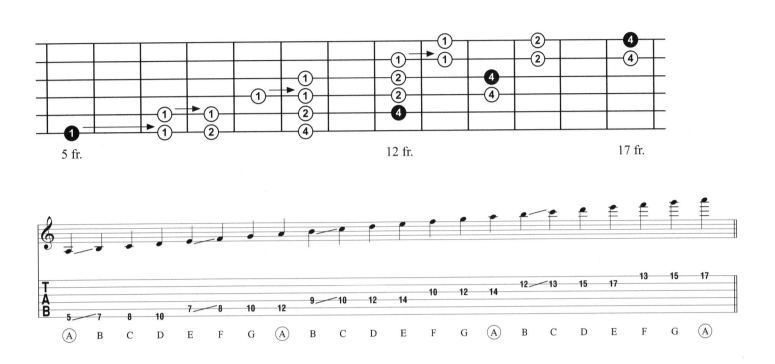

Finally, let's play the Aeolian scale in three octaves using the mirrored fingering technique. The 1-3-4 pattern is mirrored right away with a shift up on the 6th string. Notice that the second chunk of the pattern starting at the 10th fret is actually one octave of the relative Dorian scale. From there, the 1-2-4 pattern on the 4th string is mirrored again starting at the 14th fret, where we finish off the rest of the scale.

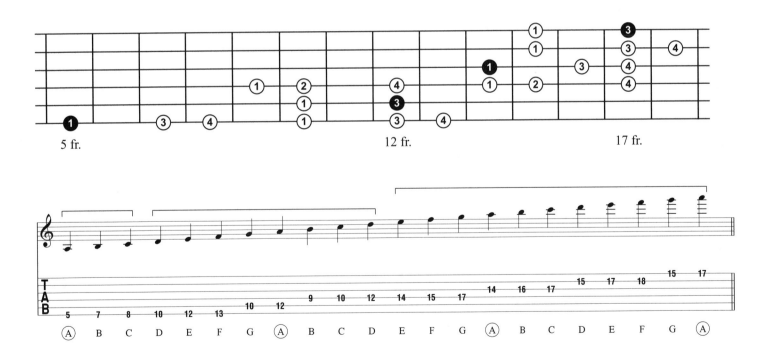

LOCRIAN MODE

Locrian Scale Patterns

Our final mode, the Locrian mode, is the most dissonant of all the modes. It can be considered a somewhat minor-sounding mode due to the presence of the minor 3rd, but the flatted 2nd and diminished 5th are what distinguishes it from the other minor modes. Because of the intervals contained in Locrian, it is believed that it was proclaimed the devil's mode and banned from use by the Catholic church. In modern heavy metal and thrash, Locrian has been used extensively, perhaps the most famous example being "Enter Sandman" by Metallica.

As with the other modes, we're going to build our Locrian scale starting on the note A. Since A is the 7th step of the B♭ major scale, A Locrian will contain the same key signature as B♭ major—two flats. Let's first look at the five scale patterns for A Locrian; then we'll explore some solos and rhythm parts.

Locrian Scale Pattern #1

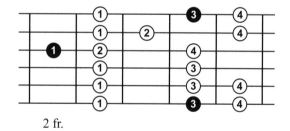

2 fr.

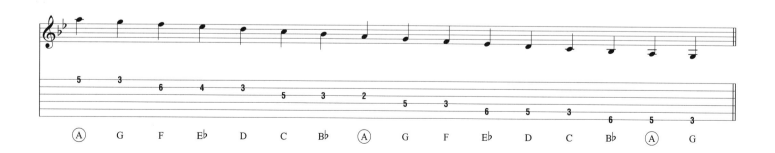

Locrian Scale Pattern #2

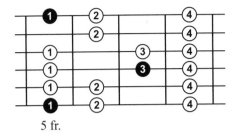

5 fr.

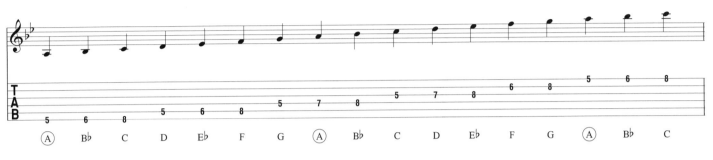

A Bb C D Eb F G A Bb C D Eb F G A Bb C

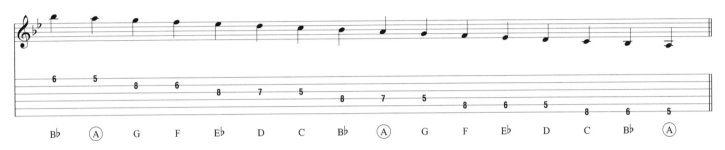

Bb A G F Eb D C Bb A G F Eb D C Bb A

Locrian Scale Pattern #3

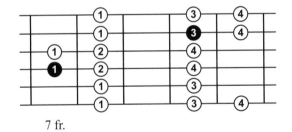

7 fr.

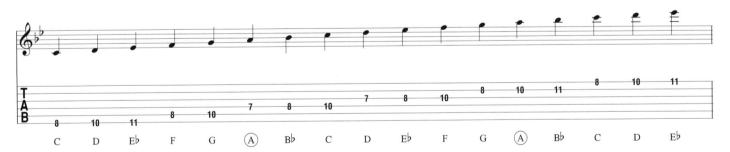

C D Eb F G A Bb C D Eb F G A Bb C D Eb

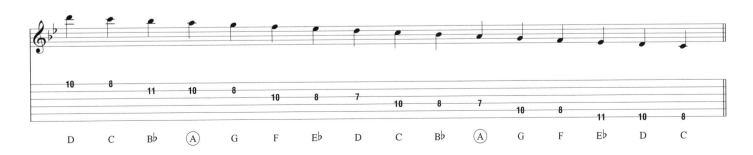

D C Bb A G F Eb D C Bb A G F Eb D C

Locrian Scale Pattern #4

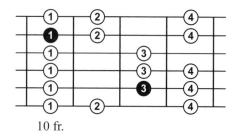

10 fr.

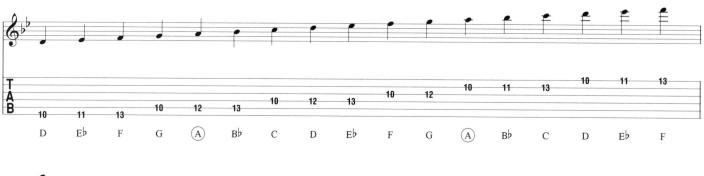

D Eb F G Ⓐ Bb C D Eb F G Ⓐ Bb C D Eb F

Eb D C Bb Ⓐ G F Eb D C Bb Ⓐ G F Eb D

Locrian Scale Pattern #5

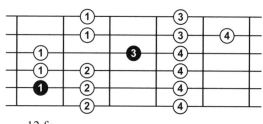

12 fr.

F G Ⓐ Bb C D Eb F G Ⓐ Bb C D Eb F G

F Eb D C Bb Ⓐ G F Eb D C Bb Ⓐ G F

Locrian Solos

Beginner Solo

Our first example is something in the style of what Tony Iommi from Black Sabbath might play. The solo starts out by making use of the ♭5 and ♭2 in a series of eerie bends with vibrato. From there, it climbs up the scale using some pull-off phrases on the 1st string to land on the tonic A at the 17th fret. The rhythm track is a fairly fast tempo with a double-time feel; practice the riffs slowly at first so you can keep up.

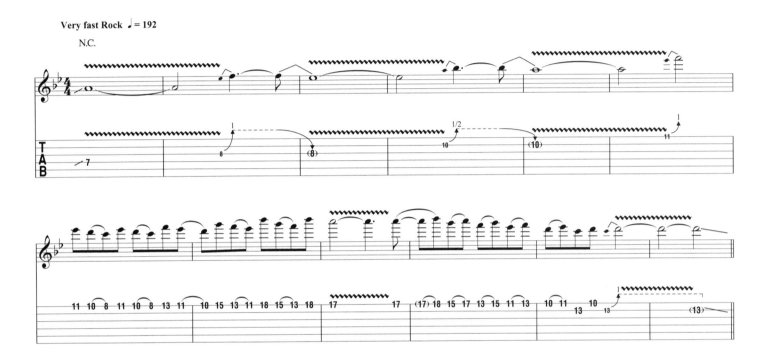

Intermediate Solo

The intermediate solo is in the style of Alex Lifeson from Rush. This is one of Lifeson's signature moves, descending down the fretboard in a series of tripet hammer-on pull-off combinations. The Locrian tonality is emphasized in the last two measures by sliding up to the ♭5 (B♭) as well as the ♭6 (F).

Advanced Solo

Finally, here's a Locrian advanced solo in the style of Judas Priest. Notice that this solo starts out with a series of bends around the pitch D. Although this note is in the scale, the relative Phrygian scale to A Locrian is D Phrygian. Locrian and Phrygian are closely related in intervals, only differing by addition of the ♭5th in Locrian. This is just another observation that can be made when analyzing these solos. The second half of the solo contains a series of fast triplet hammer-ons that incorporate a fast string skipping technique.

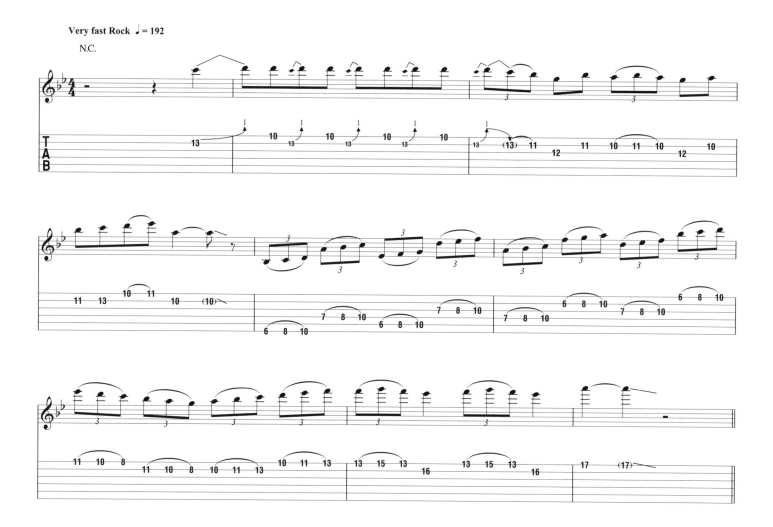

Locrian Rhythm

Writing chord progressions in Locrian is problematic due to the diminished tonic. More often than not, you'll encounter songs in Locrian keys that use single-note riffs or some power chords. We'll go ahead and harmonize the scale anyway for the sake of consistency and to also present the chords that are used in the relative keys to A Locrian, such as B♭ major, G minor, C Dorian, etc. The following charts show the triads harmonized, followed by their voicings on the guitar. Then we'll harmonize the seventh chords and show some example voicings.

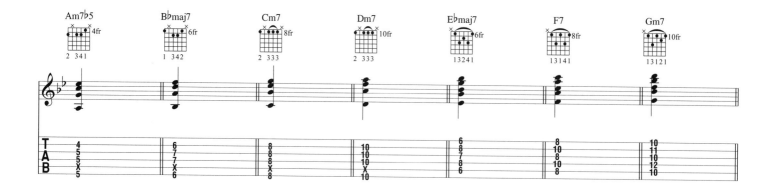

Now here's the rhythm track used for Locrian on the DVD. This is a good example of a single-note line that showcases the tonic A and incorporates the ♭2nd in the main riff. The eighth measure just before the repeat introduces the ♭5th as well, reinforcing the Locrian tonality. After the progression repeats, the last measure that makes up the second ending contains some of the power chords that can be derived from A Locrian.

As with the other minor-sounding keys, it's unlikely you'll encounter songs written with a Locrian key signature. Instead you'll probably see a minor key signature with accidentals added into the music to create the Locrian tonality. Here's a comparison between the notes in A minor and the notes in A Locrian. Keep in mind the similarity between Locrian and Phrygian as well—both are the same except Locrian contains a flatted 5th as well as the flatted 2nd.

	1	2	♭3	4	5	♭6	♭7	8
A Minor	A	B	C	D	E	F	G	A

	1	♭2	♭3	4	♭5	♭6	♭7	8
A Locrian	A	B♭	C	D	E♭	F	G	A

Now here's the A Locrian scale notated in the key of A minor with accidentals for the B♭ and E♭ on the staff.

A Locrian Scale

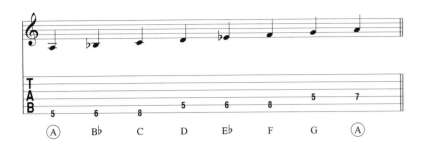

Let's also take a look at the previous Locrian rhythm track notated in the key signature of A minor (no sharps or flats). The presence of the flats on the B's and E's tells you that the music has been altered and is in A Locrian.

Most metal music you'll encounter in a Locrian key will be in E Locrian. It should look very familiar to you if you've played a lot of Metallica songs. Since the relative key to E Locrian is F major, then E Locrian would contain the same notes as the F major scale—all natural notes except for B♭. Since the key of E minor has a signature of one sharp (F♯), making it Locrian requires using naturals for the F's to achieve the flatted 2nd as well as flats for the B's to achieve the flatted 5th. Below is a typical Locrian riff written in an E minor key signature.

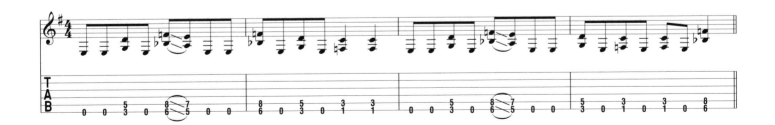

Three-Octave Locrian Scales

The Locrian scale can be a little harder to position in three octaves because of the order of the intervals. The first version below uses 4th-finger slides ascending and descending and generally tries to follow a simple 1-2-4 finger pattern until reaching the 1st string, where a wider 1-2-4 stretch is necessary. Keep in mind that the Locrian root note is only one half step below the major scale tonic; you can also just start with the Locrian root note and then follow up the relative major scale from there.

Ascending

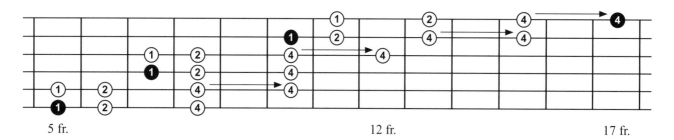

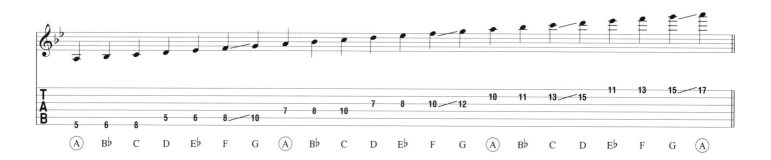

Descending

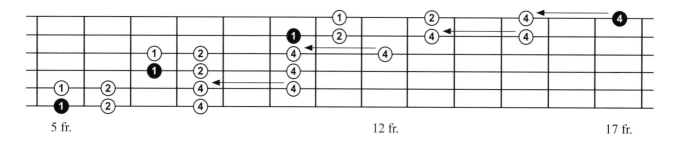

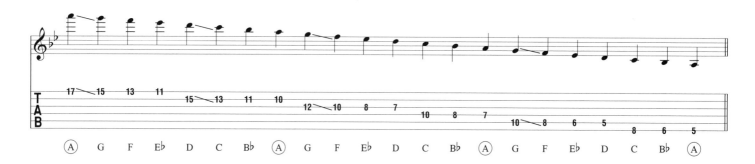

As with the previous modes, the second version of the three-octave scale contains the wider 1-2-4 finger stretches. In order to accomplish this in the Locrian mode, we've incorporated some 1st-finger and well as 4th-finger slides.

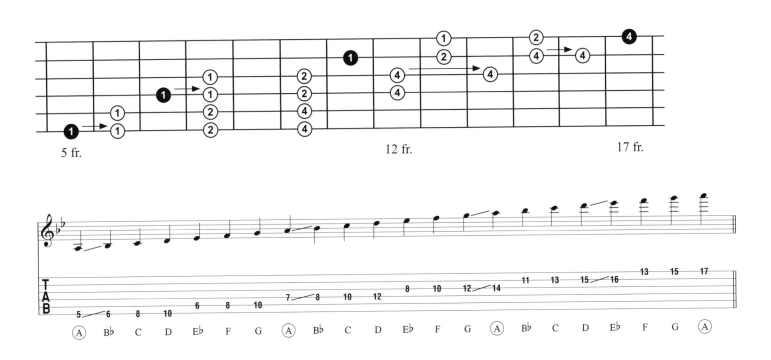

Our final mirrored fingering version of the scale breaks up the three octaves in fairly evenly distributed sections. The first position shift uses a 1-3-4 fingering on the 4th string, while the second shift uses a 1-2-4 fingering on the 2nd string.

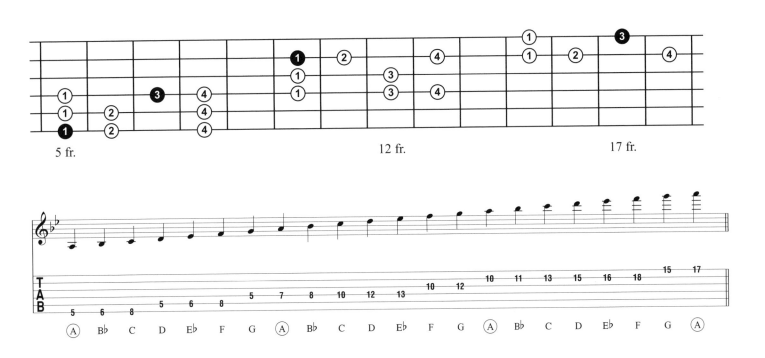

THE MODES IN NATURAL KEYS

A Modal Scales

A Ionian Scale

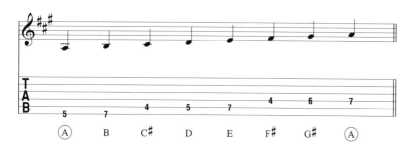
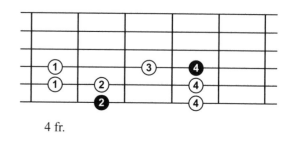

4 fr.

A Dorian Scale

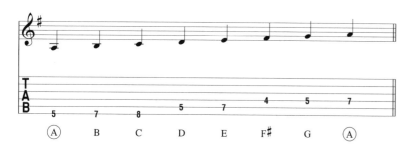
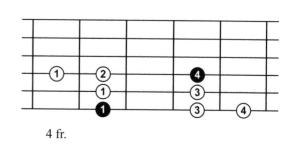

4 fr.

A Phrygian Scale

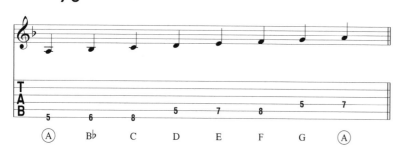
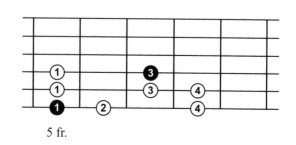

5 fr.

A Lydian Scale

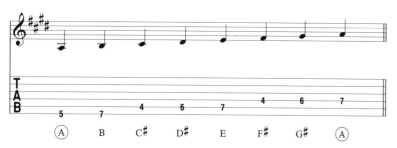
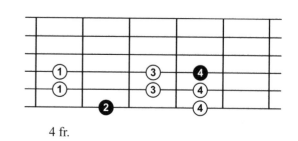

4 fr.

A Mixolydian Scale

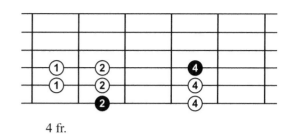

4 fr.

A Aeolian Scale

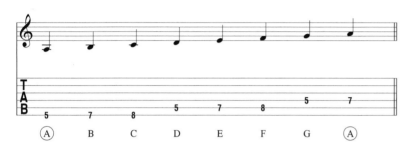

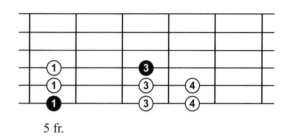

5 fr.

A Locrian Scale

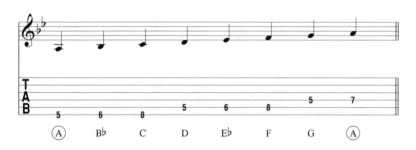

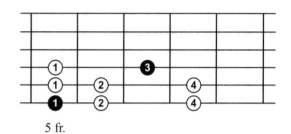

5 fr.

B Modal Scales

B Ionian Scale

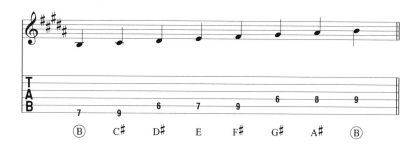

B   C#   D#   E   F#   G#   A#   B

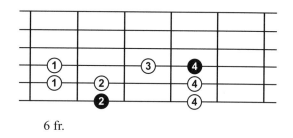

6 fr.

B Dorian Scale

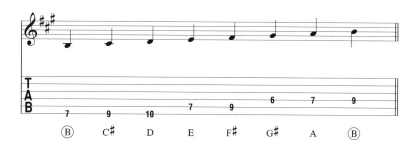

B   C#   D   E   F#   G#   A   B

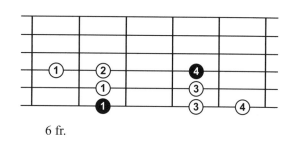

6 fr.

B Phrygian Scale

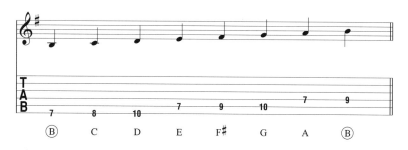

B   C   D   E   F#   G   A   B

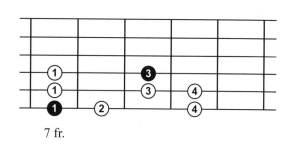

7 fr.

B Lydian Scale

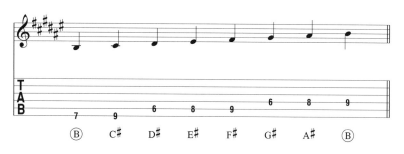

B   C#   D#   E#   F#   G#   A#   B

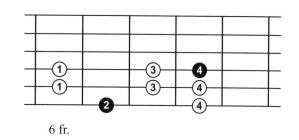

6 fr.

B Mixolydian Scale

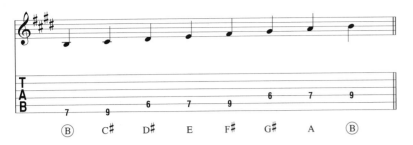
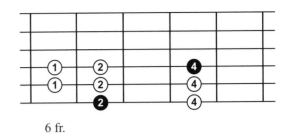

6 fr.

B Aeolian Scale

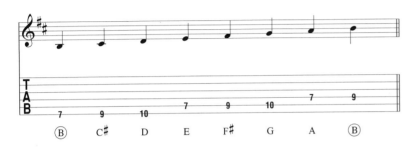
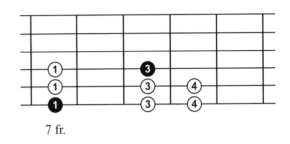

7 fr.

B Locrian Scale

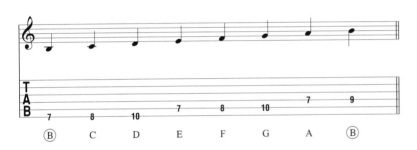
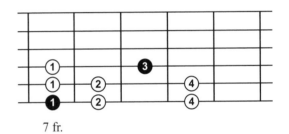

7 fr.

C Modal Scales

C Ionian Scale

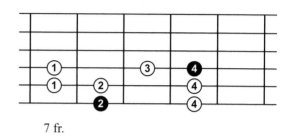

7 fr.

C Dorian Scale

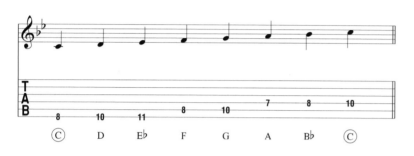

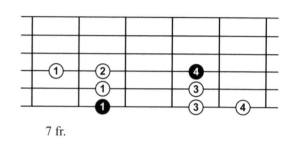

7 fr.

C Phrygian Scale

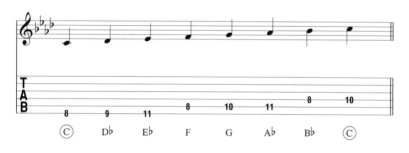

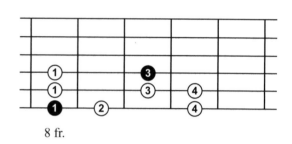

8 fr.

C Lydian Scale

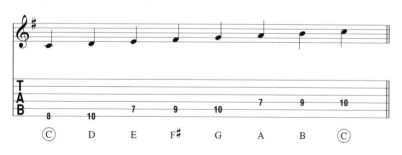

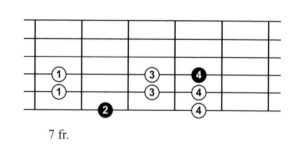

7 fr.

C Mixolydian Scale

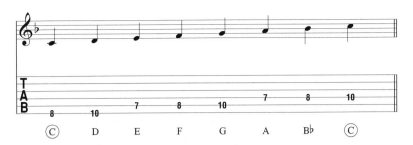

C   D   E   F   G   A   B♭   C

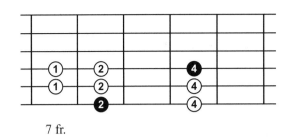

7 fr.

C Aeolian Scale

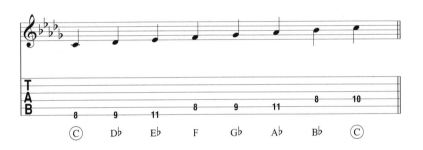

C   D   E♭   F   G   A♭   B♭   C

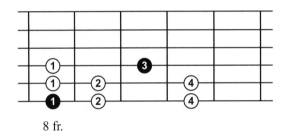

8 fr.

C Locrian Scale

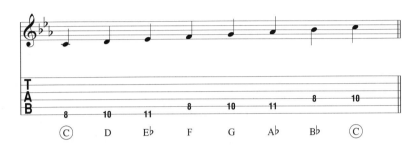

C   D♭   E♭   F   G♭   A♭   B♭   C

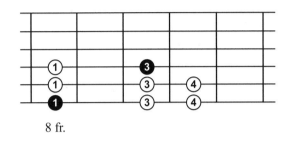

8 fr.

D Modal Scales

D Ionian Scale

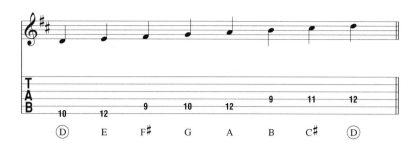
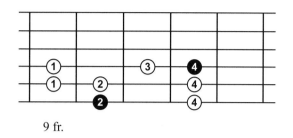

9 fr.

D Dorian Scale

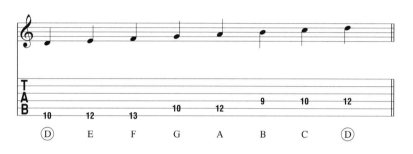
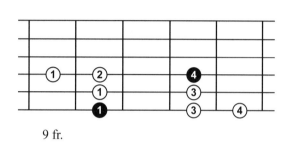

9 fr.

D Phrygian Scale

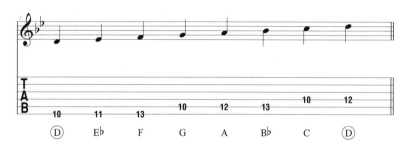
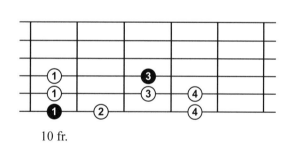

10 fr.

D Lydian Scale

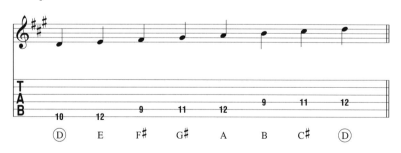
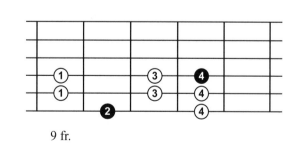

9 fr.

D Mixolydian Scale

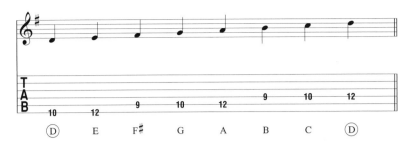

D E F♯ G A B C D

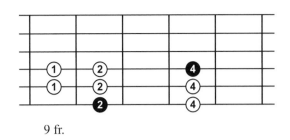

9 fr.

D Aeolian Scale

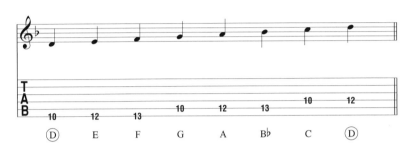

D E F G A B♭ C D

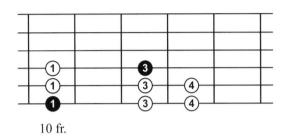

10 fr.

D Locrian Scale

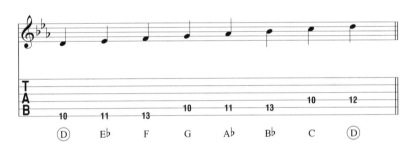

D E♭ F G A♭ B♭ C D

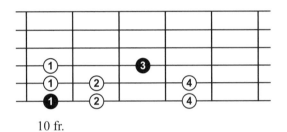

10 fr.

E Modal Scales

E Ionian Scale

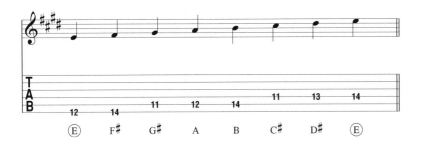

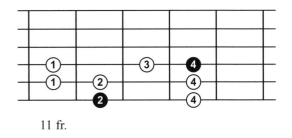

11 fr.

E Dorian Scale

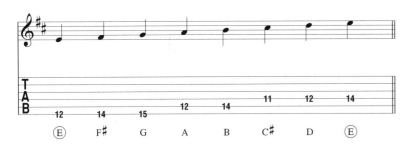

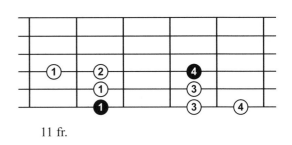

11 fr.

E Phrygian Scale

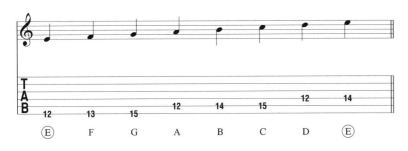

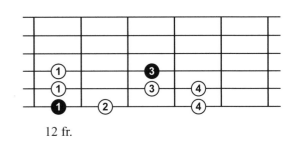

12 fr.

E Lydian Scale

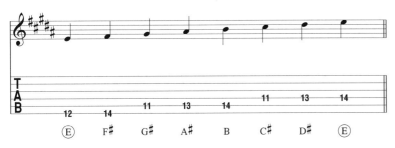

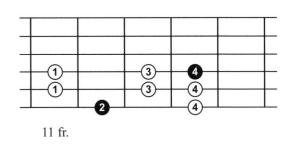

11 fr.

E Mixolydian Scale

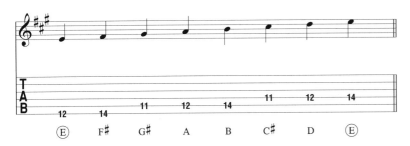

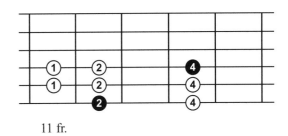

11 fr.

E Aeolian Scale

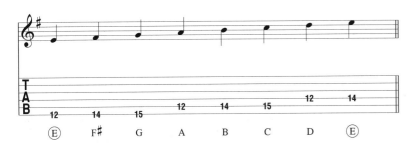

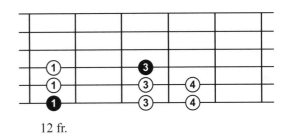

12 fr.

E Locrian Scale

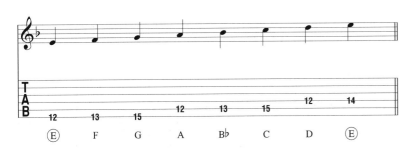

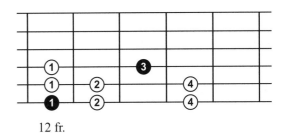

12 fr.

F Modal Scales

F Ionian Scale

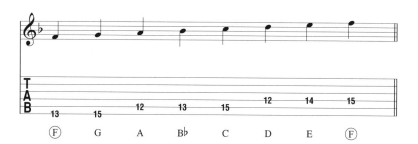

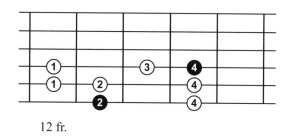

12 fr.

F Dorian Scale

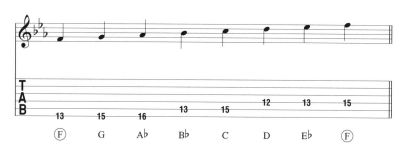

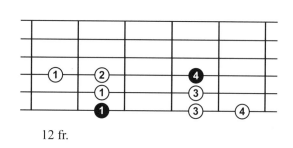

12 fr.

F Phrygian Scale

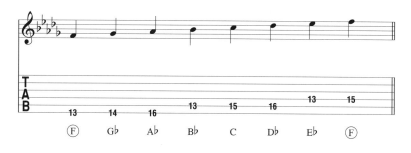

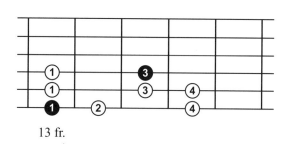

13 fr.

F Lydian Scale

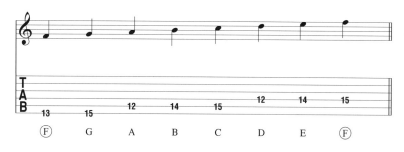

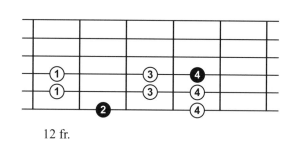

12 fr.

F Mixolydian Scale

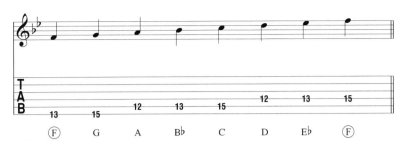
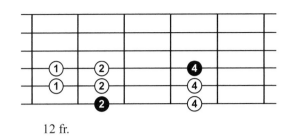

12 fr.

F Aeolian Scale

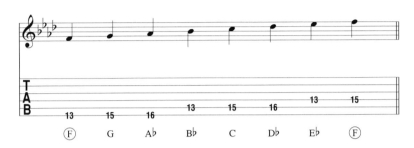
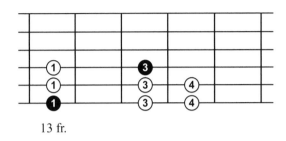

13 fr.

F Locrian Scale

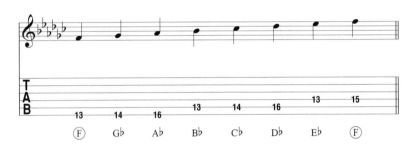
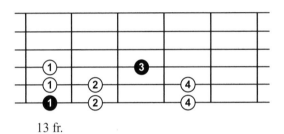

13 fr.

G Modal Scales

G Ionian Scale

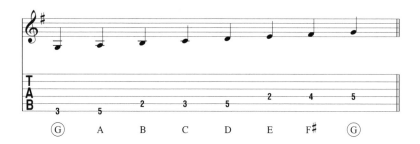

G   A   B   C   D   E   F♯   G

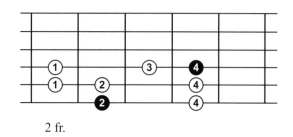

2 fr.

G Dorian Scale

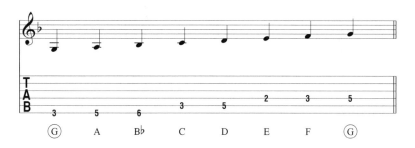

G   A   B♭   C   D   E   F   G

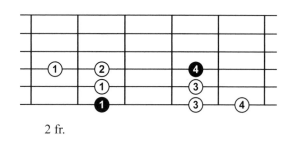

2 fr.

G Phrygian Scale

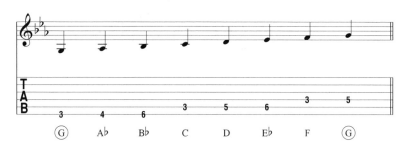

G   A♭   B♭   C   D   E♭   F   G

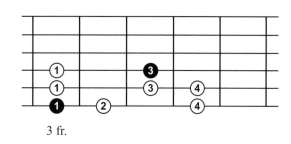

3 fr.

G Lydian Scale

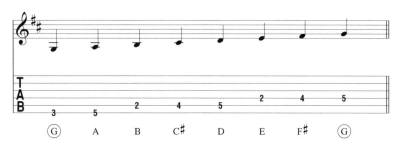

G   A   B   C♯   D   E   F♯   G

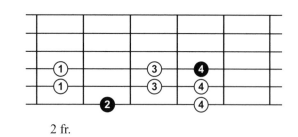

2 fr.

G Mixolydian Scale

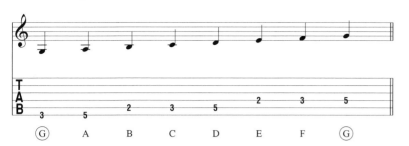

G   A   B   C   D   E   F   G

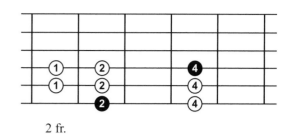

2 fr.

G Aeolian Scale

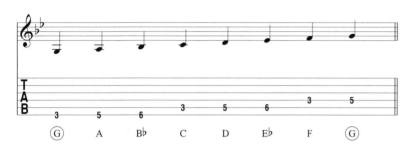

G   A   Bb   C   D   Eb   F   G

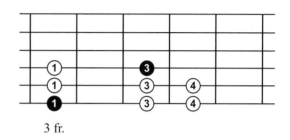

3 fr.

G Locrian Scale

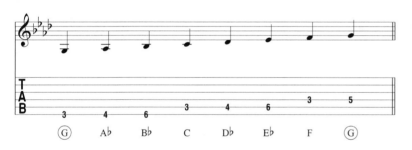

G   Ab   Bb   C   Db   Eb   F   G

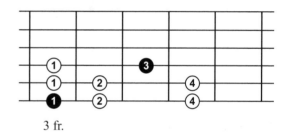

3 fr.

MODAL RHYTHM TRACKS

Here are the modal rhythm tracks from each chapter. The isolated audio tracks for these rhythms are located at the end of the DVD for you to practice soloing over.

Ionian Rhythm

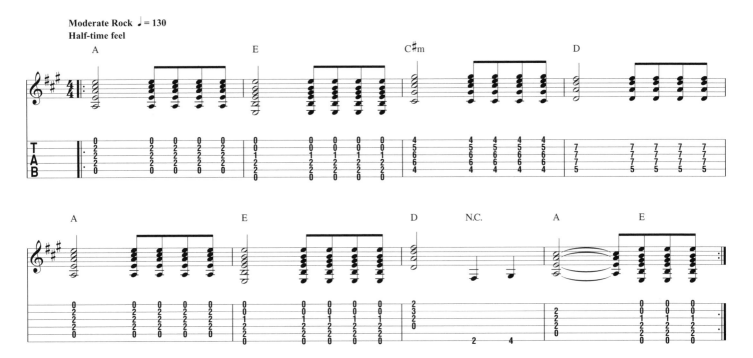

Dorian Rhythm

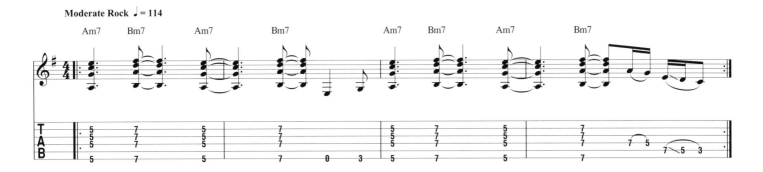

Phrygian Rhythm

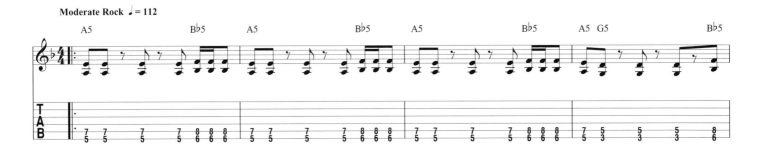

Lydian Rhythm

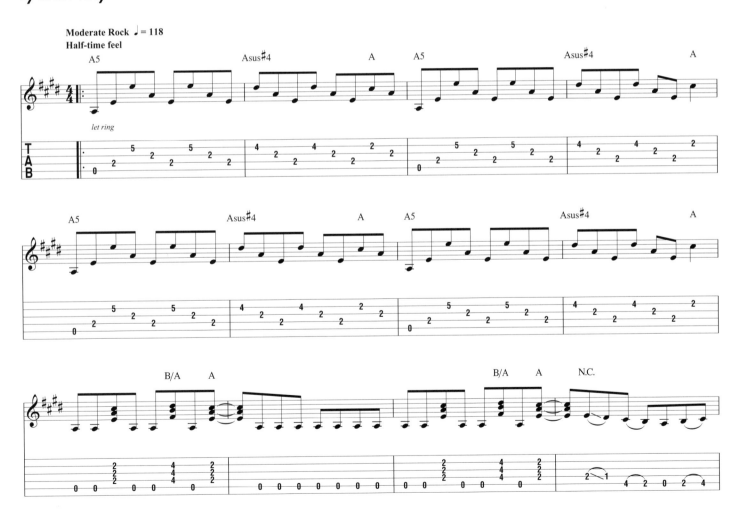

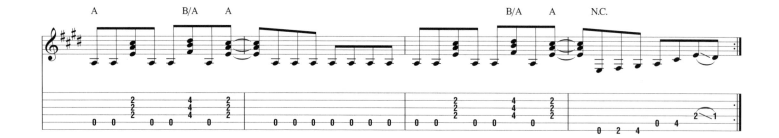

Mixolydian Rhythm

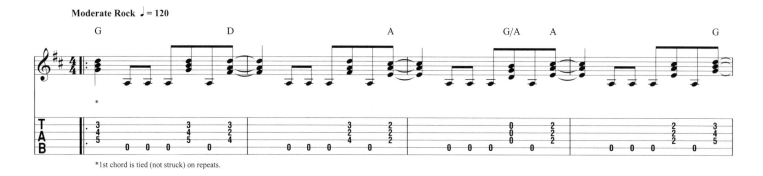

*1st chord is tied (not struck) on repeats.

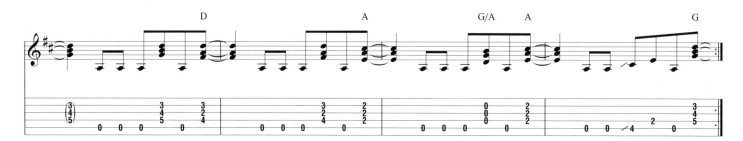

Aeolian Rhythm

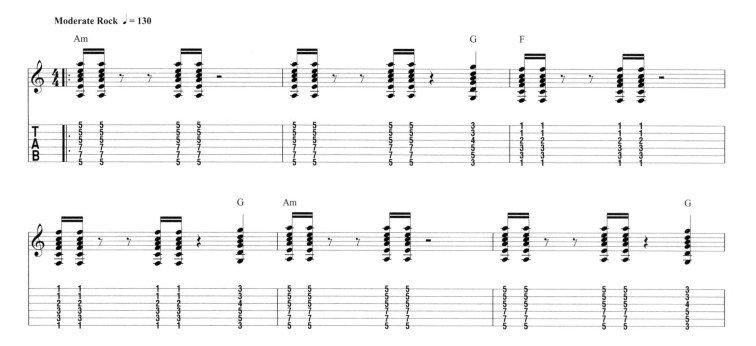

Mastering the Modes for the Rock Guitarist

Locrian Rhythm

RECORDED VERSIONS®
The Best Note-For-Note Transcriptions Available

**AUTHENTIC TRANSCRIPTIONS
WITH NOTES AND TABLATURE**

14037551	AC/DC – Backtracks	$32.99
00692015	Aerosmith – Greatest Hits	$22.95
00690178	Alice in Chains – Acoustic	$19.95
00694865	Alice in Chains – Dirt	$19.95
00690812	All American Rejects – Move Along	$19.95
00690958	Duane Allman Guitar Anthology	$24.99
00694932	Allman Brothers Band – Volume 1	$24.95
00694933	Allman Brothers Band – Volume 2	$24.95
00694934	Allman Brothers Band – Volume 3	$24.95
00690865	Atreyu – A Deathgrip on Yesterday	$19.95
00690609	Audioslave	$19.95
00690820	Avenged Sevenfold – City of Evil	$24.95
00691065	Avenged Sevenfold – Waking the Fallen	$22.99
00690503	Beach Boys – Very Best of	$19.95
00690489	Beatles – 1	$24.99
00694832	Beatles – For Acoustic Guitar	$22.99
00691014	Beatles Rock Band	$34.99
00694914	Beatles – Rubber Soul	$22.99
00694863	Beatles – Sgt. Pepper's Lonely Hearts Club Band	$22.99
00110193	Beatles – Tomorrow Never Knows	$22.99
00690110	Beatles – White Album (Book 1)	$19.95
00691043	Jeff Beck – Wired	$19.99
00692385	Chuck Berry	$19.95
00690835	Billy Talent	$19.95
00690901	Best of Black Sabbath	$19.95
00690831	blink-182 – Greatest Hits	$19.95
00690913	Boston	$19.95
00690932	Boston – Don't Look Back	$19.99
00690491	David Bowie – Best of	$19.95
00690873	Breaking Benjamin – Phobia	$19.95
00690451	Jeff Buckley – Collection	$24.95
00690957	Bullet for My Valentine – Scream Aim Fire	$22.99
00691159	The Cars – Complete Greatest Hits	$22.99
00691079	Best of Johnny Cash	$22.99
00690590	Eric Clapton – Anthology	$29.95
00690415	Clapton Chronicles – Best of Eric Clapton	$18.95
00690936	Eric Clapton – Complete Clapton	$29.99
00690074	Eric Clapton – The Cream of Clapton	$24.95
00694869	Eric Clapton – Unplugged	$22.95
00690162	The Clash – Best of	$19.95
00101916	Eric Church – Chief	$22.99
00690828	Coheed & Cambria – Good Apollo I'm Burning Star, IV, Vol. 1: From Fear Through the Eyes of Madness	$19.95
00691188	Coldplay – Mylo Xyloto	$22.99
00690593	Coldplay – A Rush of Blood to the Head	$19.95
00690819	Creedence Clearwater Revival – Best of	$22.95
00690648	The Very Best of Jim Croce	$19.95
00690613	Crosby, Stills & Nash – Best of	$22.95
00691171	Cry of Love – Brother	$22.99
00690967	Death Cab for Cutie – Narrow Stairs	$22.99
00690289	Deep Purple – Best of	$19.99
00690784	Def Leppard – Best of	$19.95
00692240	Bo Diddley	$19.99
00690347	The Doors – Anthology	$22.95
00690348	The Doors – Essential Guitar Collection	$16.95
14041903	Bob Dylan for Guitar Tab	$19.99
00691186	Evanescence	$22.99
00691181	Five Finger Death Punch – American Capitalist	$22.99
00690664	Fleetwood Mac – Best of	$19.95
00690870	Flyleaf	$19.95
00690931	Foo Fighters – Echoes, Silence, Patience & Grace	$19.95
00690808	Foo Fighters – In Your Honor	$19.95

00691115	Foo Fighters – Wasting Light	$22.99
00690805	Robben Ford – Best of	$22.99
00694920	Free – Best of	$19.95
00691050	Glee Guitar Collection	$19.99
00690943	The Goo Goo Dolls – Greatest Hits Volume 1: The Singles	$22.95
00113073	Green Day – ¡Uno!	$21.99
00116846	Green Day – ¡Dos!	$21.99
00118259	Green Day – ¡Tré!	$21.99
00701764	Guitar Tab White Pages – Play-Along	$39.99
00694854	Buddy Guy – Damn Right, I've Got the Blues	$19.95
00690840	Ben Harper – Both Sides of the Gun	$19.95
00694798	George Harrison – Anthology	$19.95
00690841	Scott Henderson – Blues Guitar Collection	$19.95
00692930	Jimi Hendrix – Are You Experienced?	$24.95
00692931	Jimi Hendrix – Axis: Bold As Love	$22.95
00692932	Jimi Hendrix – Electric Ladyland	$24.95
00690017	Jimi Hendrix – Live at Woodstock	$24.95
00690602	Jimi Hendrix – Smash Hits	$24.99
00691152	West Coast Seattle Boy: The Jimi Hendrix Anthology	$29.99
00691332	Jimi Hendrix – Winterland (Highlights)	$22.99
00690793	John Lee Hooker Anthology	$24.99
00690692	Billy Idol – Very Best of	$19.95
00690688	Incubus – A Crow Left of the Murder	$19.95
00690790	Iron Maiden Anthology	$24.99
00690684	Jethro Tull – Aqualung	$19.95
00690959	John5 – Requiem	$22.95
00690814	John5 – Songs for Sanity	$19.95
00690751	John5 – Vertigo	$19.95
00690846	Jack Johnson and Friends – Sing-A-Longs and Lullabies for the Film Curious George	$19.95
00690271	Robert Johnson – New Transcriptions	$24.95
00699131	Janis Joplin – Best of	$19.95
00690427	Judas Priest – Best of	$22.99
00120814	Killswitch Engage – Disarm the Descent	$22.99
00694903	Kiss – Best of	$24.95
00690355	Kiss – Destroyer	$16.95
00690834	Lamb of God – Ashes of the Wake	$19.95
00690875	Lamb of God – Sacrament	$19.95
00690823	Ray LaMontagne – Trouble	$19.95
00690679	John Lennon – Guitar Collection	$19.95
00690781	Linkin Park – Hybrid Theory	$22.95
00690743	Los Lonely Boys	$19.95
00690720	Lostprophets – Start Something	$19.95
00114563	The Lumineers	$22.99
00690955	Lynyrd Skynyrd – All-Time Greatest Hits	$19.99
00694954	Lynyrd Skynyrd – New Best of	$19.95
00690754	Marilyn Manson – Lest We Forget	$19.95
00694956	Bob Marley– Legend	$19.95
00694945	Bob Marley– Songs of Freedom	$24.95
00690657	Maroon5 – Songs About Jane	$19.95
00120080	Don McLean – Songbook	$19.95
00694951	Megadeth – Rust in Peace	$22.95
00691185	Megadeth – Th1rt3en	$22.99
00690951	Megadeth – United Abominations	$22.99
00690505	John Mellencamp – Guitar Collection	$19.95
00690646	Pat Metheny – One Quiet Night	$19.95
00690558	Pat Metheny – Trio: 99>00	$19.95
00690040	Steve Miller Band – Young Hearts	$19.95
00102591	Wes Montgomery Guitar Anthology	$24.99
00691070	Mumford & Sons – Sigh No More	$22.99
00694883	Nirvana – Nevermind	$19.95
00690026	Nirvana – Unplugged in New York	$19.95
00690807	The Offspring – Greatest Hits	$19.95
00694847	Ozzy Osbourne – Best of	$22.95
00690399	Ozzy Osbourne – Ozzman Cometh	$22.99
00690933	Best of Brad Paisley	$22.95
00690995	Brad Paisley – Play: The Guitar Album	$24.99
00694855	Pearl Jam – Ten	$22.99
00690439	A Perfect Circle – Mer De Noms	$19.95
00690499	Tom Petty – Definitive Guitar Collection	$19.95
00690428	Pink Floyd – Dark Side of the Moon	$19.95
00690789	Poison – Best of	$19.95

00694975	Queen – Greatest Hits	$24.95
00690670	Queensryche – Very Best of	$19.95
00690878	The Raconteurs – Broken Boy Soldiers	$19.95
00109303	Radiohead Guitar Anthology	$24.99
00694910	Rage Against the Machine	$19.95
00690055	Red Hot Chili Peppers – Blood Sugar Sex Magik	$19.95
00690584	Red Hot Chili Peppers – By the Way	$19.95
00691166	Red Hot Chili Peppers – I'm with You	$22.99
00690852	Red Hot Chili Peppers –Stadium Arcadium	$24.95
00690511	Django Reinhardt – Definitive Collection	$19.95
00690779	Relient K – MMHMM	$19.95
00690631	Rolling Stones – Guitar Anthology	$27.95
00694976	Rolling Stones – Some Girls	$22.95
00690264	The Rolling Stones – Tattoo You	$19.95
00690685	David Lee Roth – Eat 'Em and Smile	$19.95
00690942	David Lee Roth and the Songs of Van Halen	$19.95
00690031	Santana's Greatest Hits	$19.95
00690566	Scorpions – Best of	$22.95
00690604	Bob Seger – Guitar Collection	$19.95
00690803	Kenny Wayne Shepherd Band – Best of	$19.95
00690968	Shinedown – The Sound of Madness	$22.99
00122218	Skillet – Rise	$22.99
00690813	Slayer – Guitar Collection	$19.95
00120004	Steely Dan – Best of	$24.95
00694921	Steppenwolf – Best of	$22.95
00690655	Mike Stern – Best of	$19.95
00690877	Stone Sour – Come What(ever) May	$19.95
00690520	Styx Guitar Collection	$19.95
00120081	Sublime	$19.95
00120122	Sublime – 40oz. to Freedom	$19.95
00690929	Sum 41 – Underclass Hero	$19.95
00690767	Switchfoot – The Beautiful Letdown	$19.95
00690993	Taylor Swift – Fearless	$22.99
00115957	Taylor Swift – Red	$21.99
00690531	System of a Down – Toxicity	$19.95
00694824	James Taylor – Best of	$17.99
00690871	Three Days Grace – One-X	$19.95
00690683	Robin Trower – Bridge of Sighs	$19.95
00699191	U2 – Best of: 1980-1990	$19.95
00690732	U2 – Best of: 1990-2000	$19.95
00660137	Steve Vai – Passion & Warfare	$24.95
00110385	Steve Vai – The Story of Light	$22.99
00690116	Stevie Ray Vaughan – Guitar Collection	$24.95
00660058	Stevie Ray Vaughan – Lightnin' Blues 1983-1987	$24.95
00694835	Stevie Ray Vaughan – The Sky Is Crying	$22.95
00690015	Stevie Ray Vaughan – Texas Flood	$19.95
00690772	Velvet Revolver – Contraband	$22.95
00690071	Weezer (The Blue Album)	$19.95
00690966	Weezer – (Red Album)	$19.99
00690447	The Who – Best of	$24.95
00690916	The Best of Dwight Yoakam	$19.95
00691020	Neil Young – After the Gold Rush	$22.99
00691019	Neil Young – Everybody Knows This Is Nowhere	$19.99
00691021	Neil Young – Harvest Moon	$22.99
00690905	Neil Young – Rust Never Sleeps	$19.99
00690623	Frank Zappa – Over-Nite Sensation	$22.99
00690589	ZZ Top Guitar Anthology	$24.95

Prices and availability subject to change without notice.
Some products may not be available outside the U.S.A.

1113

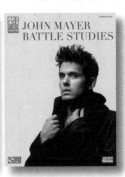

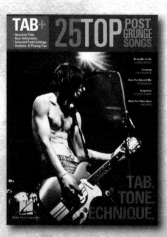